The Believer's Prophet, Priest and King

The Believer's Prophet, Priest and King

Compiled from the writings of

ANDREW MURRAY
JOHN FLAVEL

by Louis Gifford Parkhurst, Jr.

BETHANY HOUSE PUBLISHERS
MINNEAPOLIS, MINNESOTA 55438
A Division of Bethany Fellowship, Inc.

Published by Bethany House Publishers
A Division of Bethany Fellowship, Inc.
6820 Auto Club Road, Minneapolis, Minnesota 55438

Printed in the United States of America

Library of Congress Cataloging-in-Publication Data

Murray, Andrew, 1828–1917.
  The believer's prophet, priest and king / Andrew Murray, John Flavel ;
compiled and edited by Louis Gifford Parkhurst, Jr.
      p. cm.
  Revised and expanded version of Andrew Murray's Jesus Christ : prophet-
priest with the addition of three sermons from John Flavel's The fountain of
life (1671)

  1. Jesus Christ—Person and offices. I. Flavel, John, 1630?–1691.
II. Parkhurst, Louis Gifford, 1946–   . III. Title.
BT202.M88   1989
232'.8—dc19   88–33339
  ISBN 1–55661–063–7   CIP

Books by Andrew Murray

ANDREW MURRAY CHRISTIAN MATURITY LIBRARY

The Believer's Absolute Surrender
The Believer's Call to Commitment
The Believer's Full Blessing of Pentecost
The Believer's New Covenant
The Believer's New Life
The Believer's Prophet, Priest and King
The Believer's Secret of a Perfect Heart
The Believer's Secret of Holiness
The Believer's Secret of Living Like Christ
The Believer's Secret of Obedience
The Believer's Secret of Spiritual Power
The Believer's Secret of the Master's Indwelling
The Spirit of Christ

ANDREW MURRAY PRAYER LIBRARY

The Believer's Prayer Life
The Believer's School of Prayer
The Ministry of Intercessory Prayer
The Secret of Believing Prayer

ANDREW MURRAY DEVOTIONAL LIBRARY

The Believer's Daily Renewal
The Believer's Secret of Intercession
The Believer's Secret of the Abiding Presence
The Believer's Secret of Waiting on God
Day by Day with Andrew Murray

How to Raise Your Children for Christ

Authors

Andrew Murray was born in South Africa in 1828. After receiving his education in Scotland and Holland, he returned to South Africa and spent many years both as a pastor and missionary. He was a staunch advocate of biblical Christianity. He is best known for his many devotional books. He died in 1917.

John Flavel (d. 1691) was an English Puritan and Nonconformist clergyman. Educated at University College, Oxford, he was instrumental in promoting the "Happy Union" of Presbyterians and Congregationalists in 1690–1691. He is best known for his practical writings.

L. G. Parkhurst, Jr., is pastor of Christ Community Church of Oklahoma City, Oklahoma, and is the editor and compiler of the Charles Finney "Principles Series" and other devotional books for Bethany House Publishers.

God, who at sundry times and in divers manners spake in time past unto the fathers by the prophets, hath in these last days spoken unto us by his Son, whom he hath appointed heir of all things, by whom also he made the worlds; who being the brightness of his glory, and the express image of his person, and upholding all things by the word of his power, when he had by himself purged our sins, sat down on the right hand of the Majesty on high.

HEBREWS 1:1–3

The Lord Jesus Christ Prophet, Priest and King

Fullness of prophetic story,
Fullness filling all in all;
Brightness of the hidden glory,
Answer to the world's long call—
Jesus, Thou our future knowest,
Fill it with Thyself alone;
May we follow where Thou goest,
Ever Thee our Prophet own.

Great High Priest, above all other,
Sacrifice of God complete,
May we never own another,
Or confess at other feet;
Never seek another altar,
Never wish another Lamb,
Pardoned, washed, why should we falter,
Pleading in Thy Priestly name?

King of kings! may Thy dominion
Multiply and still increase;
Give Thy sway the eagle's pinion,
King of Righteousness and Peace.
Rule within Thy Church! inherit
All that Thou hast bought, great Son;
Rule o'er each blood-ransomed spirit,
Prophet, Priest, and King in One.

William Luff

Preface

*F*or many years Andrew Murray's little classic *Jesus Christ: Prophet-Priest* has blessed thousands. It was sent to Bethany House Publishers from South Africa, and was first published in 1967. The book consists of four addresses given by Murray at the Mildmay Conference of 1895. The Mildmay Conferences were commenced at Barnet, near London, in 1856, by the Rev. W. and Mrs. Pennefather, who longed for the manifestation of true Christian union. They were continued when he became Vicar at St. Jude's Mildmay Park. Murray based his speeches on Hebrews 1:1–3, and left the impression he was going to speak about Jesus Christ as Prophet, Priest, and King. However, he never covered extensively Jesus' office as King. Apparently, he covered Jesus as Prophet and Priest so comprehensively in his four lectures that he had no time left to discuss Jesus as King. When the lectures were over, it also seems that Murray did not expand his thought and bring the book to its original intended conclusion. Hence, the abbreviated title *Prophet-Priest*.

I have revised and expanded Murray's classic by including new material on Jesus as King from the pen of John Flavel. John Flavel's book of sermons, *The Fountain of Life*, (first published in 1671), includes three sermons about Jesus as King, with the traditional long Puritan titles: "Of the

11

Kingly Office of Christ, as it is executed spiritually upon the Souls of the Redeemed" (from 2 Corinthians 10:5); "Of the Kingly Office of Christ, as it is providentially executed in the World, for the Redeemed" (from Ephesians 1:22); and "The Session of Christ at God's right-hand explained and applied, being the third step of His glorious exaltation" (from Hebrews 1:3). These three sermons have been extensively edited by changing the material from third person to second person, and by updating the language considerably. They are chapters four, five, and six in this book. I believe these sermons can bring Andrew Murray's original book to a fitting conclusion, and complete the thought and teaching of Hebrews 1:1–3. Murray's final address, which would be a good communion meditation and summary, concludes this book as chapter seven.

One of my previous books, Charles G. Finney, *Principles of Union with Christ*, (Bethany House Publishers, 1985), should prove to be a good companion to *The Believer's Prophet, Priest and King*, because it covers many other titles and offices of Jesus.

As you read this book, emphasize "loving"; love Jesus as your Prophet, Priest and King. Jesus fulfills these offices because He loves us. Loving should describe our response to Jesus on a day-to-day basis, because He is *now* our Prophet, Priest and King. You might ask yourself as you read, "How does this describe Jesus' *active* love for me?" and "How can I *actively* love Jesus more in response to what He is doing for me?"

In conclusion, I wish to thank Nathan Unseth of Bethany House Publishers for suggesting that I tackle this project, for it is a joy to make valuable older writings suitable for a new readership. And I pray the same prayer that Andrew Murray used with respect to this book: "With the humble prayer that our great Prophet may use these simple words to teach His people the truth concerning himself and His blessed work. I send my loving greetings in Him to all into whose hands the little book may come."

With love in the Risen Lamb,
L. G. Parkhurst, Jr.

Contents

Christ Our Prophet

*T*he Lord Jesus Christ was God's spokesman to us, the manifestation of God to us. I have been amazed, over and over again, to read that the Lord Jesus Christ never uttered a word of His own. I have had to read it again and again, and I have often turned to see if it is really there, but in John 12:49, it is written, "The Father gave me a commandment, what I should say, and what I should speak."

Just think of it. Some of us want to be original, and say something original, to pray something original, to think something original. Oh! How ashamed we ought to be of ourselves if such a thought ever took possession of us for a moment, when the Lord Jesus was, as we understand it, never original. The Father told Him always what to say.

Yes, remember John 12:49, and do not forget John 14:10, "Believest thou not that I am in the Father, and the Father in me? the words that I speak unto you I speak not of myself: but the Father that dwelleth in me, he doeth the works." The Lord said that the words He spoke He spoke not of himself; but the Father, who dwelt in Him, He did the works.

D. M. Stearns

1
Jesus Meets My Needs

*R*ead again the first three verses of Hebrews chapter one: "God hath in these last days spoken unto us by his Son . . . who, when he had by himself purged our sins, sat down on the right hand of the Majesty on high." In these three verses, we have the three primary offices of Christ.

The prophetic office is described, "God hath . . . spoken . . . by his Son." The priestly office is described by the words, "who . . . purged our sins." And the kingly office is described by the phrase, "sat down on the right hand of the Majesty on high." The three offices are inseparably united in just the order in which they are given here.

First, by God's help, I want you to understand what it means for you to have Christ as a prophet. J. G. McVicker writes: "A prophet is a spokesman of God—one who does not speak at his own will, one who does not utter his own sentiments, but who speaks the words that God gives him to speak (Jeremiah 23:22). That was the work of a prophet— to stand in the Cabinet of Jehovah and make the people hear His words. God was the speaker and the prophets were but the mouthpiece of God." Jesus accepted His prophetic office on earth and said: "The Son can do nothing of himself, but what he seeth the Father do: for what things soever he doeth, these also doeth the Son likewise"; and "Believest thou not that I am in the Father, and the Father in me? The words that I speak unto you I speak not of myself: but the Father that dwelleth in me, he doeth the works" (John 5:19 and 14:10). The Church has Christ as her Prophet and so do we.

Our Need of Three Offices

Notice the close connection between these three offices. In the very nature of things, God planned for there to be three offices rather than two or four. Three offices are not accidental, but just what we need. We were created with a nature that has three great faculties: the power of knowing, the power of feeling, and the power of willing. Christ's offices correspond to these faculties.

First, I *know*. I am aware of the things that are outside of me. I have a sense by which I can develop knowledge of objects outside of myself. I can reason. I can see when it is dark or light. If a person is standing nearby or not, I know.

Secondly, I *feel*. Light or darkness makes a pleasant or unpleasant impression. I can feel happy or unhappy. I have emotions. I can feel good or evil.

Thirdly, I *will*. When I know something, when I know the value or the beauty of a thing, I can desire it. When it affects me pleasantly, I can choose it.

Just as there are these three faculties or powers in human beings, so God meets us with a threefold work of grace. Sin corrupts all three faculties. My understanding or my power of knowing has been darkened. My feeling or my consciousness of what I am brings me nothing but wretchedness and a sense of condemnation. Because my will has been perverted, I choose what is evil. Jesus Christ as Prophet, Priest and King meets all three needs of my being. As Prophet, He brings the light of God into my heart. He *reveals* to me my sin and wretchedness. My sinfulness is the first thing He shows me in the light of God. However, He does more than just tell me about my sin. He also tells me about God's love and the way to God. He tells me that His Father has made Him a Priest to bring me near to Him. Shining into my heart as a Prophet, He brings me to His priestly work of redeeming, purging, and sanctifying. He teaches me to understand the meaning of His work. You see the Prophet first, and then the Priest. Finally comes the kingly office. As King, He fits me to rule over sin and self.

Therefore, do not look upon the three offices of Christ as something accidental, but understand how inseparable they are to meet your every need.

The Prophetic Office Is First

Try to comprehend the truth that the prophetic office must come first. I am afraid that there is a great tendency to exalt the priestly office above the prophetic, and also the kingly office above the prophetic. I am persuaded the Church suffers immense damage from doing this. Recently I read that the priesthood is of "super-eminent importance." I do not believe it. Do not think that I do not adore and worship Christ as our ever-blessed Melchizedek; but the prophetic office must be as precious as the priestly office.

Let me first remind you of how the prophetic office always precedes the others. Look at this office throughout history. Moses was the great prophet of whom God said, "I will raise up one like unto him." There you have the prophet first, then came Aaron the priest. Later in the Old Testament, you read of the king. In the life of Jesus, the course is the same. For three years He taught and acted as a prophet. On Calvary, He began His priestly office. When He ascended, He began His kingship. The prophet must prepare the way.

Can you see why the Church can suffer much harm if she neglects the prophetic office of Christ? The prophetic office is the gate to the priestly and kingly offices. How can we enjoy the blessings of the priest and king unless we have the prophet to enlighten, lead, and teach us to take possession of what God has prepared?

Why do so many who have a strong faith in the priesthood of Christ (and praise God for that wonderful priesthood!) so often complain, "I do not realize His power. I believe in the blood, and I believe in a living High Priest, and I believe in the Holiest of all opened for me; but somehow, it has no power over me. Why does it not influence my heart and life more?" Simply because you take that truth more from the Church than from Jesus himself. You get your thought from the teaching of your mother or your minister. You do not allow the Holy Spirit himself, as the Gift of our Divine Prophet, to lead you into the blessed mysteries of divine truth in His Word.

Having a priest and a king is not enough, you must have a prophet. In the spiritual life there is not a more practical truth than this: "I must have Jesus as my Prophet." He is the Prophet of whom God said, "Hear Him." God does not intend for us to hear Him only now and then, but every day and every hour. My soul rejoices that Jesus the Prophet will reveal to me Jesus the High Priest and lead me on through the blood to His divine kingship. Beware of accounting the prophetic office of Christ as a little thing. Beware of limiting His prophetic office to the future, to prophecies with regard to the future. No, the prophet is in all things the mouthpiece of God—not only one who foretells the future, but one who tells us *how* to live.

Let me say one thing more to illustrate the truth that the prophetic office has been neglected. Do you thank God for the blessed Reformation, when the great truth was proclaimed that a person needs no intervention of a fellow man in drawing near to God, but that every anxious soul can go straight to God because the High Priest lives and is accessible to everyone? Tell me, has the great truth that you need no one, as a prophet, to intervene between Christ and you; that you can be directly taught by the Holy Spirit, been equally acknowledged and proclaimed by you?

The Uniqueness of the Prophetic Office

Tell me, from your experience and the teaching you have heard, has the prophetic honor of Jesus been maintained as well as His priestly glory? I think not. We have not honored Jesus the Prophet as we should have. The great difference between the prophetic office and the priestly and kingly offices is this: the priestly and kingly offices were fixed institutions in Israel. All the children of Aaron down through the ages were priests. Just so with the kings after Saul, they were all the sons of David, from the royal race. However wretched and ungodly they might have been, Davidic kingship was a fixed thing. But there was no race of prophets; no one could inherit the prophetic office. The prophets were raised up by God from time to time. When the priesthood and kingship failed and dishonored God, then the prophets were raised up.

In the prophetic office there is more directness of divine interposition, a dependence upon God's immediate and ever-renewed operation, with a liberty of action and progressiveness, than there is in the priestly and kingly offices. Hence, it is far easier for us to get a clearer comprehension of the priestly and kingly offices. The priestly office gives access to God, and deals with a finished work. Just so with the kingly office: Christ is seated upon the throne. The prophetic office is far more difficult to apprehend, because it implies that I must day by day in the confession of ignorance, in docility and dependence, wait upon the heavenly teaching. The prophetic office implies that each time I read one word of God's precious Word, I must ask God to let the divine Prophet speak into my ear. It implies a continuous, direct, personal relationship with God. The glory of the prophetic office has not been understood. The belief in priesthood and kingship has not exercised with sanctifying effect, because we have not waited upon Christ to reveal to us what the priesthood and kingship give.

How Christ Is Our Prophet

Let us see the way in which Christ exercises this prophetic office. Have you ever observed that when Christ spoke those wonderful words in John 14 to 17, and gave the promise of the Holy Spirit, the chief thing that He said about the Holy Spirit was something which is not ordinarily placed first? We generally think of two things in connection with the Holy Spirit: holiness (or sanctification) and power for service. But what the Lord Jesus Christ especially emphasized and repeated was this: "The Spirit will guide you into all truth." That was Jesus's chief thought.

Isn't there too much of our religion that is without this divine teaching, because we have not known our blessed Prophet, the one who teaches us each day? Let me quote from St. Paul something that will illustrate this. Remember in his First Epistle to the Corinthians, where he was telling them of Christ sending him to teach, that when Christ sent him, He gave him one warning: he must preach the Gospel, but not with man's wisdom or he would make the cross of Christ of none effect. Christ did not say, "Paul, take care you preach the cross," but He said, "Take care, when you do preach, that you do not rely on man's wisdom." Then, in chapter two, Paul goes on to tell us, "I came not with excellency of speech, or of wisdom," because Christ is the wisdom of God. You know how he had taught in chapter one that Christ has been made unto us wisdom, righteousness, sanctification, and complete redemption.

I ask you, if you have held that text in First Corinthians chapter one as a precious jewel, has the thought, "Christ is my righteousness," been far more precious than "Christ is my wisdom"? That ought not to be! If you knew what it is to bow in deep humility and set aside all human wisdom, to seek to be freed from the power of beautiful words and simply wait for the Holy Spirit to teach you, there would be new power in your preaching, teaching, and witnessing. Christ, as Prophet, does His work by the Holy Spirit.

But what is the work of the prophet? In the Old Testament, you will find the prophet has three things to do. One thing is to convince of sin. God raised up Elijah and Elisha, Isaiah and Jeremiah, Ezekiel, and all the prophets to testify against the sins of Israel, "Cry aloud, and spare not. Show my people their transgression." That is the work of the prophet.

The second work of a prophet is to reveal the spiritual truth and law of God. The prophets had to reveal the spiritual meaning of sacrifice, the spiritual meaning of the temple service and religion, and the spiritual meaning of prayer. They had to convict of sin and teach all the truth of God.

The third work they had was to convey promises with regard to the future (sometimes in the near and immediate future): promises of deliverance from the hand of enemies; promises of God's presence in the midst of His people. They were to awaken a holy expectation.

The Church Needs Prophets Today

Is not the Church of Christ in our day in need of this prophetic work of Christ? You know how He does His work. He does it through people upon earth. You have read about Aaron being a prophet to Moses. Yes, and Christ is the revealer of the heart of the Father: of God's holiness, of His love, of His saving power. Oh that God would raise up to us prophets to testify against the worldliness and sin of His people.

I remember years ago getting a letter from a missionary in Africa in which he wrote, "Would that God would raise up prophets in this world!" When every Christian and minister learns to wait upon Him as His mouthpiece, depend upon it, God will give the needful prophets and needful power to testify against sin. The work of Jesus through the Holy Spirit is to raise up prophets for the Church. Once again we need to have the spirituality of our Christian faith revealed as the prophets did it of old.

In times of decay, when the priesthood and kingship had fallen into disrepute, the prophets came to call Israel back again. We have taken too many truths from other sources than Jesus Christ himself: they have little spiritual power in our lives. But let our hearts be glad. Christ is able and willing to restore every spiritual truth of God. Christ is able to make reality of the truth which we sometimes misapprehend and sometimes rob of its spiritual power.

The work of the prophet is thus to convince of sin and to reveal the spiritual truth of God; but above all, it is his work to awaken a holy expectancy. Praise God, there are many who, when they look upon the state of Christendom, feel that we can do nothing, and yet they dare look up and believe that with God there is deliverance; their whole spirit is that of waiting upon God and hoping in Him.

If you want your heart awakened to cheerful confidence and expectancy, honor Christ the Prophet. He will show you what God can do and is going to do. Once again, Christ Jesus is the mouthpiece of God to show us all what God is preparing to do for us.

A Practical Application

I have spoken of what Christ does, but here is the practical application. What is He to be to us? Here I have just two thoughts. First, with regard to the Church in general, *let us all pray without ceasing for the Church of Christ that the prophetic honor and office of Christ may be acknowledged in its full glory.* I say it again, we all rejoice that in our Protestant churches there is no more thought of a priest intervening between our souls and God: Christ himself sprinkles us with the blood. We may, indeed, have direct communion with God: direct teaching and guidance from Jesus Christ. Let us pray to God that in the work of the Church this blessed truth may be brought forth in its fullness, that everyone may have direct contact with Jesus—not only the saving Jesus, the redeeming Jesus, but also the teaching Jesus.

Let us pray that God will give to all of His ministers of the gospel, all faithful preachers of the gospel, and all Christian witnesses a right sense of their holy position. Christ, the mouthpiece of God; I, the mouthpiece of Christ. I pray you, if you are to honor Jesus as the Prophet, as the mouthpiece of God, then you must live toward Him as He lived toward God. You must give yourself to prayer in continuous waiting, in quiet self-abnegation and trust, to be taught by Him through the Spirit. If you pray thus, Christ the Prophet will use you as He has perhaps never done before.

My second thought is a word to all individual believers. Beloved, it will have profited us very little to have only heard *about* Christ. We will have gained very little from knowing the fulfillment of the prophetic word, if we are content to have only the thought of what the word prophesied in the past, and how it has been fulfilled. We need something more: *we need the living Christ himself.* Christ's installation as Prophet was beside the Jordan when He was baptized, and God declared, "This is my beloved Son." So, listen to Jesus, the living one. "Hear ye him." Christ, our heavenly Prophet, can descend and come down into our whole life. With every spiritual perplexity we feel, with every prayer we send up, with every difficulty in our daily path, He can be our Teacher.

Let Jesus be your Prophet, let Him be your Teacher. Wait on Him: "They that wait on the Lord shall never be ashamed." Above all, if you are longing that He should lead you into the mysteries and blessedness of the priesthood, into the very Holiest of all, within the veil, there ever to dwell in God's light—if you would have Him lead you into the faith, the experience and the joy of the ransomed, and enable you to sing every day, "Now unto him who loved us, and washed us from our sins in his own blood, and . . . made us . . . priests unto God," then let Jesus, as the Prophet, come in. Bow before Him even now, yield yourself to Him, rejoice in Him, and trust Him.

E. A. Stuart has written: " 'No man hath ascended up to heaven but he that came down from heaven, even the Son of man who is in heaven.' That is to say, all other human prophets have been, as it were, trying to reach up to heaven, and directly they have got to the mountain height, and God has given them a direct revelation of His truth, they have come down again and made known that revelation. But no man has ascended up to heaven to get the whole revelation, save He who came down from heaven. This is why the Lord Jesus Christ is a true Prophet—because He is the Son. In John 1:18, we read, 'No man hath seen God at any time; the only begotten Son which is in the bosom of the Father, he hath declared him.' And it is because He is the Son of God, because He was in the bosom of the Father, therefore, He is that Prophet that should come into the world."

Christt
Our Priest

What a wonderful Savior the Lord Jesus Christ is! Each new glimpse that we get of His glory seems to be brighter and better than anything we have ever seen before. When He comes to do any work of grace in our hearts, it seems the very best that He can do for us. So, when we hear of our Lord Jesus Christ as the Prophet, we are tempted to exclaim, "Surely this is His most wonderful office! Surely there can be nothing in Christ that goes higher or is more glorious than His work of revealing God the Father!"

When we turn to speak of Him as the Priest, we cry, "God forbid that I should glory, save in the cross of the Lord Jesus Christ." When we see Him as our King, we fall in adoration at His feet, and crown Him Lord of all. So we need to be reminded that we must not set any one of these offices against the other, for the whole Jesus is fully in each of them.

But our subject now is the priestly work of the Lord Jesus; and what I would say to you is this: Give yourselves up for a while in the adoration of our Lord Jesus as Priest. Be content for the time being to think of this as His most wonderful work, and ask God that the glory of it may break afresh upon your soul."

G.H.C. MacGregor

2
Fellowship With God

*R*ead the first verse of the eighth chapter of Hebrews: "Now of the things which we have spoken this is the sum [the Revised Version says, "this is the chief point"]: We have such an High Priest who is set on the right hand of the throne of the Majesty in the heavens." Our High Priest is Jesus Christ, the completion of sacrifice and priesthood.

The object of priesthood is the restoration of fellowship with God. The priest was to take the sinner into God's presence. What is spirituality then? We have just as much spirituality as we have of God. Becoming more spiritual, which is revival, means nothing but this: to get more of God's will, more of God's presence, more of God's power.

Priesthood means simply this: the bringing of us into perfect fellowship with God. See how this is illustrated in the story of Israel. Look at Exodus 25:8; just where God begins to give Moses His command about the tabernacle and the priesthood. He has spoken of the freewill offerings, and then follows: "Let them make me a sanctuary; that I may dwell among them." God wanted to live near, to live with, to live among His people. He wanted His people to live with and near Him. Look at chapter 29. There we have it more distinctly connected with priesthood. In verses 44 and 45, we read: "I will sanctify also both Aaron and his sons, to minister to me in the priest's office; and I will dwell among the children of Israel, and will be their God." Priesthood has no purpose apart from God's dwelling among His people.

And now in the New Testament, the great object of the priesthood is this: that we may dwell with God every hour of our lives and that God may dwell with us and in us. We should ever go back to Calvary and the atonement, to the Cross and the precious blood, to look at the everlasting foundation of our hope. When, however, a person has laid a foundation, he does not always abide there; but he builds up and up and higher until the superstructure is complete. Calvary and the Cross are our foundation. But what is the house that God has built upon that? What is now the life into which God leads us through the Cross and Calvary? The answer is found in a study of all that the priesthood implies.

Our High Priest Is God and Man

Everything must commence from Jesus the High Priest. Then we can go on to see a little of His work as High Priest in heaven; and after that, what that work will accomplish for us in the world.

Why is Jesus Christ such a perfect High Priest? The Epistle to the Hebrews tells that He is God and He is man. As God, He is the omnipotent Creator—not only holy, righteous, and able to conquer sin outside of us, but as Creator-God He has access to our inmost being, so that He can indeed cleanse us and lift these hearts of ours into fellowship with God.

But He is not only God, He is also man. We see in that beautiful fifth chapter of Hebrews the two great thoughts connected with His humanity. First, that He himself was perfected in obedience by His suffering and His struggle. He learned obedience; and so, as our High Priest, He can teach us obedience. And when He, as High Priest, gives us His Holy Spirit, the Spirit that He gives us is the very Spirit of the obedience that was in Him. Let us take that in.

The very essence of Christ's work on Calvary is obedience to God. He gave himself up to the will of another—not His own will, but the will of His Father. And when Christ, as Priest, brings me up to God, it is by the divine Spirit that He gives me the same mind and disposition as was in Him during His earthly walk.

Second, we see in His humanity the deep tenderness with which He sank down into perfect conformity with us, into all our tears, prayers, and sufferings. And therefore I may have great confidence that there is no place in which I am and no condition in which I suffer but that the High Priest is willing to enter into its depths, to make himself one with me and, in it and through it, to lift me up to God.

Oh, brother and sister! My Christ is *God*! Mystery of mysteries! Jesus Christ is my Christ—my Christ is a *man*—a man as I myself am. The Epistle to the Hebrews tells how Jesus Christ as man, having finished the sacrifice for us, went up to heaven and now has a heavenly priesthood. There He carries on the priesthood in divine and everlasting power. It is this heavenly priesthood of Jesus Christ we want to think of. This is the sum of all that is written here and throughout God's Gospel. "We have such an High Priest who is set down at the right hand of the throne of the Majesty on high." Christ is a heavenly High Priest who gives us a heavenly life and enables us to lead a heavenly life on earth.

The Minister of the Sanctuary

What is the work that He does as this great High Priest? He brings us nigh unto God. In connection with that, there is a double work spoken of in the eighth chapter of Hebrews. If you read this chapter carefully, you will find that Jesus Christ bears two names: the one name is the "Minister of the Sanctuary;" the other is, the "Mediator of the Covenant." These two names are linked together inseparably. And we need both.

What do I understand when I read that name, "the Minister of the Sanctuary"? In every temple there is a god, an unseen god, to whom the temple is devoted. But there is also a priest, the priest of that temple, who is to receive the petitions or the sacrifices of the worshiper and to get the answer back. So it was with Aaron. It is said of him and of the priests in Israel, "they shall stand in my presence to minister," and "they shall go out and bless in my name."

Redemption is Godward and manward. Jesus Christ stands as the Minister of the Sanctuary in His Godward work and as the Mediator of the Covenant in His manward work. What does that mean? Christ, as the Minister of the Sanctuary, has first of all opened the sanctuary by His blood. When He ascended into heaven He entered with His own blood into the Holiest place. With that blood, with that sacrifice—the better sacrifice—the heavenly things were all cleansed. In opening the Holiest with His blood, He secured us complete and totally confident access into God's presence. He is the Minister of the Sanctuary.

But Jesus Christ is more. He lives there that He may ever act for us and do the work of bearing us up before the Father. He prays. It is written, "He liveth to pray." These are not prayers with words, not prayers such as ours; but His whole being, His presence before God, is one unceasing intercession. Without ceasing there rises from Him to the Father a cry that never fails, a cry for more of the Spirit, more life, more blessing, and more of the love of God to be manifested in the Church of Christ here on earth. And without interruption, there flows back from the Father to the Son, in whom He delights, a stream of blessing to impart to His Body upon earth.

And even so, there flows forth unceasingly from the Son a stream of blessing unto His believing people. It is flowing even now. Do try and realize this. Just as the sun does not exist for one moment without pouring out its light, so our Lord Jesus cannot exist—I say it with reverence—cannot exist one single moment without the love, Spirit, power, and blessing of God flowing out from Him. If we would learn to believe in the power of that intercession, we would live more joyfully. We could heartily sing, "To him that loveth us, and loosed us from our sins by his blood . . . to him be the glory and the dominion!"

Now, the Priest not only opened the temple, and He not only dwells there as an intercessor—He does more. He brings us in. He has told us in His Word that we all are to live in the Holiest of all. You know the text: "Having therefore, brethren, boldness to enter into the holiest . . . let us draw nigh." Alas! our hearts are so foolish, so feeble, and so ready to fail that we too often think, "I cannot enter into that holy place, and I never could expect to be always kept abiding there. How could I, with this sinful nature, always, without ceasing, live in the house of God, in the presence of the thrice Holy One?"

Here comes the blessed thought to help us: Christ is the Minister of the Sanctuary. He is there to take us in, to bring us in, to keep us in, to take us ever deeper in. He is there to watch over us and to instruct us, and to guide us every hour. Oh, beloved, learn to understand what the author of the epistle means when he writes, "Having boldness to enter into the Holiest of all." Believe that you have a High Priest over the house of God, a Minister of the Sanctuary, into whose keeping God will give you. "Let us draw nigh." We can enter with Jesus, the living Jesus, who will bring us in.

Another work of the Priest is to communicate to us all the blessings that we are to receive as we tarry in the Holiest of all. What is it that I am to do when I am in the Holiest? I am there to learn about worship. To learn what it is to sink down into ever-deepening humility before God. There I am to be clothed with the likeness, the spirit, and the beauty of Jesus. There I am to receive afresh, everyday, the overflow and the inflow of the Holy Spirit from my beloved Head.

How can I attain to these things? Beloved fellow believers, you have a High Priest who waits every moment to do His perfect work in you. All that you long for as you tarry in the Holy Place, you may count upon Jesus, the High Priest, to do for you in power. Let us take to heart this one work of Christ: "He died, the just for the unjust, that he might bring us unto God"; or as in Hebrews seven: "A better hope whereby we draw nigh to God."

The great goal of the priesthood of Jesus is to bring us nearer to God. You know *practically* just as much or as little of the priesthood of Jesus as you have of the nearness of God. Does your heart long for deeper fellowship with God? We have often sung "Nearer, my God, to thee." But take again today, with large faith, the blessed truth of the work of the High Priest, the God-man Jesus. His work is to bring and to keep me near to my God. I can count upon Him to do it. Will you count upon Him for that? Let every heart say, "Amen, I will trust Jesus to keep me near to God." And then, whatever desires you have, whatever needs you feel, whatever hopes arise in you, depend upon the fact that Christ will and Christ can fulfill them all.

Now we know what it means to say that He is the "Minister of the Sanctuary"—the Minister of that heavenly place into which we are to go and where we are to live. But now comes the great difficulty. We cry, "Alas, my sinful heart! How can I ever hope to live all day in the presence of my God, in the Holiest of all! Here is my feeble nature, here is my faithless heart, and here, too, are my circumstances, so trying and full of temptation. For hours and hours I am often compelled to concentrate all the attention of my mind and heart on some worldly business. I do it in the Lord's name, and yet my heart is occupied with these things." Listen, brother, while I tell you of the other name of Jesus: "He is the Mediator of the New Covenant."

The Mediator of the New Covenant

Christ is "Mediator of the New Covenant" because He is more than the surety of the Covenant. Even that word "surety" means more than we think. At the beginning, He was my surety when He paid my debt; but that was only the beginning. Christ is my surety that the Covenant will be fulfilled in me. He is my surety for what I need today. And He is that surety because He is the "Mediator of the New Covenant."

Do you know what that New Covenant is? Have you read the beautiful account we have of it from Jeremiah in Hebrews eight: "Their sins and iniquities will I remember no more." That is the first part; but there is a second: "I will put my laws into their mind, and write them in their hearts." Then, there is the third: "They shall not teach every man his neighbor, and every man his brother, saying, Know the Lord: for all shall know me, from the least to the greatest."

The work of our High Priest is to see that the New Covenant is fulfilled. He must mediate, come down from heaven, to continually secure and make actual in my heart the reality of forgiveness and pardon far beyond feeling, and to make plain to me that every time I fail I can get pardon again. Christ can, by His Spirit, lead us into the wonderful power of His blood, so that we may know what it is to have a constant trust in Him and to have no more remembrance of the sin that has been put away. Christ Jesus is able to make the power of His blood such a reality that the life of God can shine unbrokenly in my poor heart.

In chapter nine of Hebrews, just where we read of Christ's entering the tabernacle and the Holiest with His blood, there is reference to the human side of spiritual cleansing: "How much more shall the blood of Christ cleanse your conscience from all dead works, to serve the living God?" Oh, have you such an apprehension of what Christ's blood can do? Do you long for it? There are no words that fill me more with wonder and admiration than that precious phrase, "the blood of Christ." Oh, let us know that blood which our High Priest applies. Let our souls rejoice in Him. Let us ask Jesus to keep us in the full enjoyment of this first blessing of the Covenant.

Then comes the second blessing, "I will write my law in their hearts." Praise God! What does it mean to have a law in the heart? It means this: To have the knowledge and the will and the power of God's law inspired into us. For example, when I speak of an acorn, how do I know that it will grow up into a mighty oak tree that may stand for a hundred years? Because the law of the oak tree is written in the heart of the acorn. The acorn may be small and the resulting oak may be spreading its branches for a hundred years to come, but it was all in the acorn. Even so with Christ. My High Priest is to see that the Spirit of the Lord God shall live in me, rule in me, conquer in me, and work out all His blessed purposes in me. Christ, the High Priest, is Mediator of the Covenant for this blessing too—a life that lives out the law written in the heart.

And now let us consider the last blessing—immediate

and unbroken fellowship with God. The prophet leads us on into the fullness of the blessing: "A man shall not need to say any more to his brother, Know the Lord," for there will be direct, immediate, personal communication between God and the soul. "All shall know him, from the least even to the greatest." Beloved, Christ is the Mediator of the Covenant. He is not only Minister of the Sanctuary in heaven, but also the Mediator of the Covenant on earth.

Just think, for a moment, why these two things must go together. That will make clear to us the blessedness of this priestly work. We know that every creature is designed according to the kingdom to which it belongs. A plant belongs to the vegetable kingdom, an animal belongs to the animal kingdom, and each must have a constitution according to the nature of that kingdom. Take an ox. Why is it that you can nowhere make an ox so happy as in a field of rich grass? A lion would not be at home there to find its food, nor would a man. But the ox nature and the grass are suited to each other. Why are some people, when brought into rich homes, made unhappy? Because their nature is accustomed to wretchedness and poverty. Why did Jesus say to Nicodemus, "Except a man be born again, he cannot enter the kingdom of God"? It was for the same reason. I must have a nature in harmony with the Kingdom.

And now, what good is it that Christ is the Minister of the Sanctuary, that the most wonderful promises are open to me, and that I may enter into the Holiest of all, if I have not the power, the sympathy, the heart that is prepared to dwell there? Sometimes Christians have read those promises almost with despair. They have said, "It is not for me; my heart is not fit for it." But let me tell you, Jesus Christ taught us to pray, "As in heaven, so upon earth," and He works it himself. As Minister of the Sanctuary, He keeps heaven open for you every moment; as Mediator of the Covenant, He is fitting you every moment for it. If you will trust Him and His blood to cleanse you, He is willing to breathe the law of God into you, and He himself is willing to be the bond of fellowship with God. May Christ make the covenant a reality in your life. I fear we too often look at Jesus as an outward Savior. We think of Aaron and what he did with the blood of bulls and goats, and then we multiply that work of mediation by millions and millions to understand Jesus' work. There is no comparison. Christ's blood is divinely precious, and Christ himself is the divine Savior; but still we do very little else than magnify the work of Aaron into immensity or infinity to compare. We do not know what the absolute difference is; that the work of Aaron was an outward work, and the work of Christ is an inward work.

The sun is many hundreds of thousands of miles away from us, but on a cold day you go out and say, "I am going into the sun." And the sun actually comes into you and passes through your marrow and blood, warming that which was benumbed and ready to freeze and die. In the same way, my Lord Jesus is in inconceivable glory. But by His divine grace He is the Mediator of the Covenant, and I can come not only into His presence as He is in heaven, but the light and warmth of His love can shine into me, even here upon earth! He is fitting me, as a poor, sinful child of the world, to walk with God, to enjoy real and true fellowship with God, to dwell in the love of God, and to follow Him.

Oh, friends, we do not understand the words we use when we speak of these things! They are too high and too wonderful. But, still, let us use them all the same, and let us pray to God to make His wonderful redeeming love our full and daily experience. Let Jesus be our High Priest—the Minister of the Sanctuary, opening heaven to our hearts; the Mediator of the Covenant, opening our hearts for heaven to enter in and fill them.

What is all this to end in? What is the object of all this? Is it done so I can live in God's presence and be very happy and very holy? No. These things are but the means to an end. What is it then? It is that I, like Christ, should also be a priest.

Our Priesthood

You all know that wonderful thought connected with Aaron. God made Aaron high priest in such a sense that his life carried priesthood to all his descendants. Through fifteen hundred years a descendent of Aaron was priest, because he was a son of Aaron. The life of Aaron carried the blessing. But consider the life, the divine life, of my High Priest! Do you think that His life would carry less blessing than the priesthood of Aaron? Certainly not.

Time will not allow me to allude to the deep meaning of the priesthood of Melchizedek—one who never dies but lives in the power of an eternal life, working every moment. We have that precious word in Hebrews seven: "He was made a priest after the power of an endless life." Yes. Jesus Christ imparts His own life to us. I have referred already to what we see in Exodus—the priesthood, the means of the indwelling. In Hebrews five, it is said that Jesus Christ did not exalt himself to be High Priest, but God said unto Him, "My Son, this day have I begotten thee."

The priesthood of Christ! Is that a dead doctrine? No, indeed. The priesthood has its root in sonship. The divine life of the Son is what gives the priesthood its power to bring us nigh to God—to bring us into His life, and His life into us. It means that all the love and holiness of God dwells in the Son. Sonship means that when He takes us up and we are made partakers with Christ, we not only get an external pardon but we get the Holy Spirit within us. Jesus, the High

Priest, does His work within us. He gives us His own life. We cannot have the benefit of the priesthood in full power except as the power of regeneration works and Jesus comes as the indwelling one to reveal himself. If we begin to understand that, then we shall understand why we are all called to be priests, because we have the very life of the High Priest in us—not only imputed, but the High Priest himself dwells within us.

The Purpose of Priesthood

And that brings us to the concluding thought. Believers, I ask you all, why are we considering the priesthood of Jesus? Is it only that we can know better how our sins can be blotted out and conquered? Is it only because we want to know better how we can enter into the Holiest and dwell there in the full light of God's love? If so, there is a basic misunderstanding of the priesthood.

What does priesthood mean? Self-sacrifice to the death for God and for man. That was the spirit of Jesus, and that is the spirit that Jesus wants to breathe into every priestly heart that is willing to yield itself to Him. Oh, brother, He, through the eternal Spirit, gave himself up to God, a sacrifice without spot. And when I receive of that eternal Spirit into me, the priesthood of Jesus becomes a reality and the double work that Jesus does becomes my work too. Praise God! It becomes your work. And what is that work, that double work? You go even into the Holiest of all as an intercessor.

I could say much about this blessed subject if I had time. Every Christian should get more definite training from Christ in the work of intercession. Let me say a word to all who have the command of their own time. Have you ever thought about the fact that in heaven Jesus has the command of His own time and that He spends it in unceasing intercession? "He ever liveth to make intercession for us." Have you ever thought of the glory that this gives to prayer?

If this day you claim afresh the priesthood of Christ as your only hope, then pray for the spirit of intercession. By the grace of God, begin to pray more for the perishing world around you, pray for Christ's feeble, sickly Church, pray for God's servants in Christendom and in heathendom. Live in this faith: "I have become united to the High Priest, and He has given me a priestly heart that intercession might be made not only at times but continually from me and from every member of the Body."

I said that with the priest in Israel there were two thoughts: "he shall stand before my face to minister" and "he shall go out to bless the people." That is what Christ does: He intercedes above, and He sends the blessing down. That is the double work every priest has to do: to ask and bring down the blessing from above, and then go out and dispense it. I know it is the prayer of many an earnest heart: "God, help us that this may not be a time of spiritual self-indulgence. God, help us that we may not be feeding upon old or upon new truth while our hearts do not beat for our fellow creatures."

We have spoken about the High Priest who gave up His place upon the throne and came to this earth to give His life and His blood. There is a place for you on earth with Him and in Him. Give yourself up to follow Jesus, even to Calvary.

Oh my High Priest, breathe Thy Spirit into me! Breathe Thy priestly Spirit into me! I am a member of the Body; I have Thy life in me. Like Thee, I am a priest. I am Thine! Holy Jesus, breathe Thy Spirit into me and let me only and ever be with Thee that Thou mayest be glorified and my fellow men blessed.

God will make the blessing ours.

3

Into God's Presence

*O*h, the blessedness of a life in the Holiest! Here the Father is seen and His love tasted. Here His holiness is revealed and the soul made partaker of it. Here the sacrifice of love and worship and adoration, the incense of prayer and supplication, is offered in power. Here the outpouring of the Spirit is known as an everstreaming, overflowing river, from under the throne of God and the Lamb. Here the soul, in God's presence, grows into more complete oneness with Christ, and more entire conformity to His likeness. Here, in union with Christ, in His unceasing intercession, we are emboldened to take our place as intercessors who can have power with God and prevail. Here the soul mounts up as on eagle's wings, the strength is renewed, and the blessing and the power and the love are imparted with which God's priests can go out to bless a dying world. Here each day we may experience the fresh anointing, in virtue of which we can go out to be the bearers, the witnesses, and channels of God's salvation to men, and living instruments through whom our blessed King works out His full and final triumph. "Oh Jesus, our great High Priest, let this be our life!"
—*The Holiest of All*

Let Us Draw Near

In Hebrews 10:19, you find these words: "having therefore." With this verse the second half of the epistle begins, and that "therefore" sums up the whole previous nine chapters. "Having therefore, brethren, boldness to enter into the holiest by the blood of Jesus, by a new and living way, which he hath consecrated for us, through the veil, that is to say, his flesh; and having an High Priest over the house of God; let us draw near." The one lesson of the epistle as of the whole of Holy Scripture is: "let us draw near." The work of the priesthood is to bring us near to God. "Let us draw near with a true heart in full assurance of faith, having our hearts sprinkled from an evil conscience, and our bodies washed with pure water. Let us hold fast the profession of our faith without wavering (for He is faithful that promised) and let us consider one another to provoke unto love and to good works; not forsaking the assembling of ourselves together, as the manner of some is; but exhorting one another; and so much the more, as ye see the day approaching."

The words from which I wish to speak are in the nineteenth to the first half of the twenty-second verse, and especially these words, "let us draw near." These words are not addressed to the unconverted. They do not speak of conversion. They include that, but they are spoken to Christians, to the Hebrew Christians. Believers are told: "Let us draw near." The text supposes that there are believers (and the Hebrews were among them) who did not live as near to God as they might. They had wandered, they had not been diligent in pressing on to the fullness of gospel truth, and they were not living in nearness of God. A child can be a dear child and yet be far away from the father. "Let us draw near." The message is especially to believers.

It does not mean "let us draw near in prayer." It is often

so understood and, indeed, is applicable to prayer; but it means far more. I cannot be praying the whole day, in the sense of speaking to God. I have my business to attend to—and God wants me to work and be just as near to Him as I engage in business as when I pray. "Let us draw near" is meant to cover the whole life—every day and every moment. It is not a nearness of thought. I can think, imagine, and argue that Christ's blood is shed, that there is access for me, and that I have the right of coming nigh; and yet, I may be only thinking and arguing about the nearness of God without really living and enjoying it. No, the phrase means actually, experimentally, and spiritually: "let us draw near to God." It does not mean that we should draw near *sometimes*. It means, as with a child who has wandered from his father, that we should draw near and abide near. Nearness to God is the great blessing of our High Priest: let us take it and use it. We read in Ephesians: "We have been brought nigh by the blood of Christ." Let us live in that nearness to God.

If we want to obey this command, we ought to set before us very distinctly what our life ought to be. We have access into the Holiest. The Holiest is now to be our home. Just a word about that. God wants us to live every day and all day in His holy presence. Where God is, there it is heaven. The presence of God means heaven; and God is omnipresent. We all believe that. And the difference between an unconverted man and the believer is this: the unconverted man does not recognize the presence of God, while the converted man often thinks of it and desires it—too often, however, only as a passing thought or relevant subject. But the man who goes on to perfection, according to the teaching of the epistle, accepts and claims the abiding presence of his God as his continuing unchanging experience.

Are there any hearts longing to abide in God's presence without interruption, without a break? You say, "That is impossible. My business, my duties prevent it." No, I want to make you understand that the presence of God is something He will take care of. He will take care that you shall have it, whether you keep thinking of Him or not. Look at the sun, and look at the people in the street. Have you seen any of them taking the trouble to secure the shining of the sun? No, the sun shines without their concern or mine. God makes sure that the sun shines; the sun takes care that there is always light flooding us. We only have to come out into the light and enjoy it. And will God not take care that His light always shines upon us? If we fully believe that, I think one great difficulty will be out of the way.

People always think, "What can I do?" and "Shall I really be able to live this way?" My brothers and sisters, come today and think of what God can do. God can do wonders. We have just to draw near, trust, and give up ourselves to lead this blessed life. When we wait upon and trust Jesus, the great High Priest, He will make His presence a reality.

You complain of your feebleness against sin. I want to lead you to a place today where God will enable you to conquer sin. This place is the Holiest of all, His presence. You complain of your feebleness in work. I want to lead you to a place where God will breathe His Spirit upon you every day and give you new strength for work. You complain of so many difficulties and troubles. The Father has prepared a home for you, a resting place, in His own home, in His very presence. Do you believe it? Do believe it! And Jesus, the doorkeeper, the Minister of the Sanctuary, the Priest in the Temple, will bring you in and teach you how to have the love that always pleases God.

The Holiest Is Open to You

Now, let us look at the four great arguments found in the verses preceding the command, "Let us draw near"—the four great arguments to encourage us to draw near. First, "having boldness to enter the holiest." The Holiest is open to you. Second, "having boldness by the blood." The blood gives you the boldness. Third, "having a new and living way." The way will carry you to the Holiest. Fourth, "having a High Priest over the house of God." The High Priest will watch over you. Now, let us draw near.

First of all, the Holiest has been opened up to you, "having boldness to enter the holiest." You know from your Bibles what the Holiest was in the tabernacle. The tabernacle consisted of two rooms or compartments. One (we may call it the front one) was where the priests lived and served. They were allowed to walk in and out continually in the service of God. The other room (the back compartment) was separated from the front one by a thick veil. There God dwells in a cloud, between the cherubim on the Ark of the Covenant, and no one was allowed to enter through that veil or look behind it on penalty of death.

Just think what an extraordinary thing this is. God has said, "I want to come to my people, to dwell among them, and I want to let them dwell with me." But He (I say it with reverence) shut himself up in a dark place, and no one could come to see their God or meet Him. Only the high priest might enter in, and then only once a year for a few minutes. But he had to go out again, at once; and if he or any priest entered in at other times, immediate death was the punishment. God had His abode, but written over that abode were these words: "No admission on penalty of death." For fifteen hundred years God kept the people away from direct contact with himself.

But what happened? All at once the veil of the temple was rent in two from top to bottom. The amazed priests, who were in the holy place, saw the Holiest of all opened up. They rushed out with terror and fear lest they should die. How did the curtain tear? At that moment, Christ had died. His death and His blood rent the veil and gave access into God's presence. What does that mean? Does it mean only that Christ should, fifty days after His death, ascend to heaven and enter within the veil? Thank God it means that! But there is a great deal more. It means that you and I are called to enter inside the veil. When? Not at death, but now—now, by union with our living High Priest, by faith in the love of God that has welcomed us to Him.

Brother, if you had been a priest in Israel, would not your heart sometimes have longed, "Oh, that I had the privilege of the high priest to go into God's very presence!" And yet you would have thought, "It is only for a moment, even the high priest has to come out again." There hung that veil, God's great object lesson, for fifteen hundred years. People could not come too near to God. The Israelites were allowed to come into the outer court, and their priests into the holy place, but no one could come too near to God.

The veil is now rent, and the command comes to you to come into the most complete and intimate nearness. God wants His children, by the Holy Spirit, to draw very near, to enter and to dwell in His very presence. I ask you, do you believe God means it? It is the place prepared for us.

When a man comes from a long journey, having been absent for years, his mother will prepare a room for him with loving care. And when he comes, the mother says, "Here is your room. See, we have made it nice for you. You must come and stay here now." Today God comes and says, "My children, I have prepared the best room for you. The place where I dwell, there you must dwell."

The place where Jesus entered with His blood, there you can enter. You must enter! He says, "I want you to enter in and dwell in my love." Oh, come, let us draw near. If there are any whose hearts tell them, "Alas! I have not been living

52

in this union. I am no nearer to God now than in the days of my conversion. I have known what it was to believe, but into this abiding union, into this daily experience of the presence of God resting upon me from morning till night, I have not entered"—to you comes the message: "Let us draw near." What will be your answer? "Blessed Father, I come, take me in."

Have Boldness by the Blood

Secondly, "having boldness by the blood." I know the great difficulty that troubles you. The thought runs through many a heart, "Oh sin, sin, sin! With a fallen nature it is impossible always to be dwelling in the Holiest of all." Listen now! "Having boldness to enter in by the blood"—oh that God might reveal to us what that means! I am afraid you do not give the blood of Jesus the honor that God means you to give it. God honors that blood as infinitely, inconceivably precious. To Him, Jesus' blood is worth more than anyone can tell—the obedience of His beloved Son! Oh! that we would take the trouble to find out, "What is that blood worth to me?"

In Israel, what honor they gave to the blood of a lamb or a heifer! In connection with Christ's blood, we read in Hebrews of cleansing by the ashes of a heifer. A heifer was sacrificed and the blood of that sacrifice sprinkled before the tabernacle of the congregation. The heifer was then burned with other items and the ashes kept for purification. When a person touched a dead body, he was unclean. The prepared ashes were then mixed with pure water and sprinkled upon the person. What happened next?

Up to the time that he was sprinkled, he was kept out of the fellowship of God's people, and out of the court; but when he had been sprinkled he was clean. He then proved his trust in the blood of the heifer by boldly coming back and taking his place as a cleansed and restored person. He was restored to his people and to the presence of God.

The blood of the sacrifice was of such value to the unclean person that even the ashes of the sacrifice were considered sufficient for cleansing. If the blood and the ashes of the heifer were considered cleansing agents, I ask, what honor ought we give to the blood of the Son of God?

You tell me, "I cannot understand all that the Bible teaches about the cleansing of the blood. I hear differences in expressions used. Tell me, what does it mean?" God forbid that you should wait for this! Do not seek to find your rest in different expressions of belief, or in having your own correct theory. But, I pray you, if you have any difficulty at all, come at once. Faith is something far beyond understanding. Honor the precious blood by believing that the blood can bring you nigh and the blood can keep you nigh. Say today, "However sinful I feel myself, that is not going to keep me back from trusting God! The blood—the blood of Jesus—is my boldness and my confidence."

"Having boldness by the blood"—I want you for a moment to try to realize what that means. What is the worth and the power of that blood? When Christ approached heaven as the Mediator and Surety of guilty sinners, and when He asked entrance into heaven not only for himself but for all those who should believe in Him, what was the answer given at the gate of heaven? If there had been an angel doorkeeper to ask, "How canst thou demand access for all that guilty race?" the answer of Jesus would have been, "My blood is their ransom! I have conquered sin. I have made an end of it and put it away. I have satisfied the Father. I have access to the Father." And, oh, if Christ went in for us by His blood, shall we not honor the blood? Shall we not trust the blood? Shall we not say in the midst of all difficulties, "I cannot understand or explain all, but I can trust the infinite power of the blood of the Lamb. This is my boldness!"

Oh, beloved, believe in that blood today; honor it, even now, by boldly claiming your place in the nearness of God. That blood is able not only to bring you in now and again, but it is the blood of the sacrifice, shed once for all and forever. And in that everlasting power, it can keep you ever abiding in God's presence. Ask Jesus, by the power of His Holy Spirit, to make the cleansing of your heart with that precious blood a living reality, truth, and life; and the blood will be your boldness every moment. It will give you confidence to say, "I can dwell with God all day. As long as the blood speaks for me, I may confidently claim the everlasting and ever abiding nearness."

A New and Living Way to the Holiest

Then comes the third argument, "having a new and living way." The Holiest is opened up and we are given boldness through the blood, but there is also, "a new and living way," the way that Christ opened up "though the veil, that is, through his flesh." In other words, the new and living way is the way of the cross, the way of death.

In Christ's death on the cross, God condemned sin in the flesh. The flesh was the veil that separated Christ from God. He had dwelt with God, but He came outside the veil and lived a life of trial, temptation, prayer, struggle, and faith. His flesh was, in a very real sense, the veil between God and man. But Christ rent that veil by giving His flesh to be rent and broken on Calvary. This is the way of the rent veil. The flesh given up to the will of God, even to death, is the new way He opened up.

In the beginning of Hebrews ten, you will find that the old way was "by sacrifices," the sacrifices of animals; but

Christ came, and in doing the will of God He opened a new and living way. And now, dear Christians, here comes the most difficult part. There are many Christians who long to enter into the presence of God, but they do not want to come by the new and living way. They think a great deal about the blood, the title and right it gives them to enter in, but they do not understand this way by which we must walk. Christ is the Way. That means in the way in which He lived, I must live; in the way in which He walked, I must walk.

Are you willing to draw near to God in the way in which Christ drew near to Him? Understand, the nearness of God is not a thing of *locality*; it is a thing of *disposition* and *will*—it is a *spiritual* thing. I may be sitting next to a person and yet in heart and inclination, I may be far from him, abhorring what he thinks about. Another person may be far away from me, say in South Africa, and yet I may be in the most intimate nearness with him in love, in similarity of disposition and purpose. And so the nearness of God is a nearness of life, a nearness of sympathy, a nearness of love.

Here is the new and living way by which I have come: giving up my will in obedience unto death. The blood has set the door wide open, but there is a way in which we must walk. Christ is my living path and my living leader, and it is as I give up my will and my life in self-sacrifice—like Christ—that I draw near to God.

Oh Christians! I am afraid there is a great deal of comfortable Christianity that wants to be converted, to be saved, and to be made happy; but it is not the Christianity of Christ. The Christianity of Christ means that you must give up everything to God. It means that you must give up your whole will to God. It means that you must give your life a sacrifice to God every hour of the day. Christ's call is: "Let a man deny himself, and take up his cross, and follow me."

There are Christians who do not want to walk in that

path of self-denial. I dare not say how a man ought to sacrifice himself; but I dare say this, the true believer will be asking God often, "Oh my God, what would You have me sacrifice more for your sake?" Remember that prayer. Walk in the path of Jesus. Pray often, "Lord, teach Your people, and teach me to know what the new way is that Christ opened—the way of death unto life, the way of obedience into glory, the way of humiliation into the highest exaltation."

You say, "This is a hard saying. All that you told us about the Holiest of all opened up was beautiful; and all you said about the blood was precious; but now it becomes too hard for us. We are weak, and cannot walk the way of Christ." Listen now to what the Word says to meet your difficulty. The new way is a *living way*. What does that mean? All our paths and streets are dead ways. If I have not the strength to walk along the street, the street will not carry me. If the car or train or bus has not some power to move itself, the street will not move it. These ways are all dead.

But, praise God, there is one living way. It is this: when a poor, helpless sinner, who cannot move a foot, casts himself upon Jesus to become conformable to Him; gives up his heart and will, and chooses to walk in the self-sacrifice of Jesus; then the Way takes him up and lifts him on. What is that living way? It is the power of the Holy Spirit of Jesus.

Listen, Jesus did not walk in that way, go to heaven and leave me behind *in my own strength* to walk like Him. Never! Jesus went to heaven and then sent down the Holy Spirit by whom He had walked in the new way. The Holy Spirit will strengthen me, so that in Christ, who is the Way, I walk even as He walked. The way is a difficult one, a hard one, a way of submission, humiliation, and death. But, thank God, it is a living way if we but once surrender ourselves to it. The Spirit of God will be our strength and our joy.

Our High Priest Will Give Us Boldness

And then, lastly, "and having an High Priest over the house of God." We have had three great lessons, three great motives, for drawing near; but the fourth is the best of all. I have had the Holiest of all set open. I have had the blood given me as my assurance every hour and every moment. I have had the new way set before me as a living way, that from hour to hour will carry me. But yet I have not all I need. The last is the best: the living person of my living Lord Jesus Christ.

"Having an High Priest"—just think of that word "having." We *have* "such an High Priest." How have I? In thought? He is in heaven, and I have Him here? Ah, no! I have a house in South Africa, but I cannot enjoy it today, for I am here in England. And many people have Jesus as their Savior in heaven, but so little do they enjoy Him here. But here, praise God, we have the liberty to say we have a High Priest in personal enjoyment. How can that be? I can have Jesus in no other way than in my heart. I cannot have Him with my hands, my mouth, my eyes. My thoughts have not a spiritual and divine object. My thoughts can think about it, but they cannot have it. But the heart! Oh, that I could tell every believer, "With your heart you have Him." Occupy yourself more with this blessed truth, and believe it out to the very end. I have the Almighty God, the great Priest, the living, sympathizing Jesus, over the house of God. I have Him—not a bit of Him, not something of Him, but the whole undivided Almighty Jesus. I have Him, praise God.

Oh, souls, take time to believe this. Take time to worship until your heart is filled. I have a great High Priest to watch over this wonderful life in the sanctuary. I have Jesus; and when sin comes, He makes everything right up above as well as here below and within. I have Jesus, and He leads me along that new and living way. I have Jesus within my heart. I have Him and hold Him. I love Him and trust Him. Jesus Christ does indeed bring me into the presence of God. When it cost Him the agony of Gethsemane and the death on Calvary, He did not refuse; but He went to the very uttermost that He might open it up to me.

And now that the price is paid, the blood shed, the door open, and the heart of the Father made glad, will my Lord Jesus refuse to take me in? God forbid that such a thought should enter our hearts! Jesus lives to take us in and to keep us in.

Now, what is to be the fruit of our meditation upon the priesthood of Jesus? Is it to be this, that from today you will live nearer to God, more full of the joy of His presence? Is it that from today you will honor the blood as you have never honored it before, to bring you deeper into the inner sanctuary? Is it that from today you will give up yourself to the new and living way, the way of self-sacrifice in the power of the Holy Spirit? Is it that you will learn to trust Jesus and give yourself entirely to Him that He may do His work in you and bring you nigh to God? Oh, beloved, the High Priest does this work by dwelling in the heart. Come, let us now open our hearts wide to Him. Oh, come, and as we have gazed upon His work—from Calvary to the throne of glory, and from the throne back again into our hearts, and from our hearts back again to the presence of God into which He brings us—let every heart say, "Jesus, I have *You*! I have *You*!"

Beloved Christians, accept Jesus now with a new acceptance. Take hold of Him now with a new hold. "Jesus, Minister of the Sanctuary, High Priest, and King, I have You, I have You! And You have me, Lord, and we will never part. I am linked to You by the power of Your blood!" And having Jesus as our High Priest, let us draw near, let us draw near, let us draw near!

"The joy of our Lord's inner life was in love, in the love which always pleased the Father, which always obeyed His will, which always lived in His presence. And in the same proportion that we have fellowship with Him in this—for He puts before us no lower standard, but calls us into the same relationship with himself as He had with the Father—shall we have fellowship in His joy. When the soul is brought into conformity with Jesus, there is the sunshine of God's smile without a cloud between. The law of holiness is the law of joy."—*Mrs. Pennefather.*

Christ
Our King

*J*esus comes as King to those of us who believe in Him. He comes in to set up His government and write His law within our hearts. He comes to establish His kingdom within us, and to sway His sceptre over our whole being and personality. He must be spiritually revealed and received by us personally as our great and glorious King.

We need Him to reveal himself to our souls as the one upon whose shoulders rests the government of the universe. Jesus is the King! He governs this world for the protection, discipline, and benefit of all believers in Him. This revelation of Jesus as King has a powerful sin-subduing tendency in the hearts of those who honor Him as their King. We will tend to live a more humble and obedient life for our King when we know that all events are directly or indirectly controlled by Him. We praise Him knowing that absolutely all things are designed for and will surely result in our good.

Charles G. Finney

4
Spiritual Blessings

We now come to the *Regal Office* by which our glorious Mediator executes and discharges the design of our redemption. If He had not, as our Prophet, revealed the way of life and salvation to us, we could never have known it. Since we cannot know salvation apart from Him, it is also true that if He were not our High Priest and had not offered himself up to obtain redemption for us, we could not have been redeemed by His blood. If we have been redeemed, still we need Him to live for us in the capacity of King, to apply this purchase of His blood to us so we can have actual, personal benefit by His death. For what He revealed as a Prophet and purchased as a Priest, He applies as a King.

As our King, He subdues our souls to His spiritual government. Then He rules us as His subjects, ordering all things in the kingdom of Providence for our good. Jesus Christ has a twofold kingdom: one is *spiritual* and *internal*, by which He subdues and rules the hearts of His people; the other is *providential* and *external*, by which He guides, rules, and orders all things in the world in a blessed subordination to their eternal salvation. I desire now to tell you about the spiritual and eternal kingdom from the text: "Casting down imaginations, and every high thing that exalteth itself against the knowledge of God, and bringing into captivity every thought to the obedience of Christ" (2 Corinthians 10:5).

Paul's words in our text are considered two ways, either *relatively* or *absolutely*. Considered relatively, they are a vindication of the apostle from the unjust censures of the Corinthians, who, very unworthily, interpreted his gentleness, condescension, and winning affability to be no better than a fawning upon them for selfish ends, and the authority he exercised no better than pride and imperiousness. But here he lets them know that as Christ did not need such carnal tricks, so he never used them either: "*The weapons of our warfare are not carnal, but mighty through God.*"

Absolutely considered, his words hold forth the efficacy of the gospel in its plainness and simplicity, for the subduing of rebellious sinners to Christ. In this sense, we have three things to consider.

First, we must understand that sinners use *oppositions* against the assaults of the gospel through *imaginations* or reasonings. Paul means the subtleties, slights, excuses, subterfuges, and arguings of fleshly-minded people in which they fortify and entrench themselves against the convictions of the Word of God. Yes, and there are not only such carnal reasonings, but many proud, high conceits with which poor creatures swell, and scorn to submit to the abasing, humble, self-denying way of the gospel. These are the fortifications erected against Christ by the carnal mind.

Second, we must understand the *conquest* which the gospel obtains over sinners who are fortified against it. The gospel casts down, overthrows, and takes high places and strongholds. Thus Jesus Christ spoils Satan of the chance to show the sinner that all this can be no defense of his soul against the wrath of God.

Third, we must see beyond the immediate *victory*. Jesus

Christ did not only lead away conquered enemies, but brings them into obedience to himself. After conversion, He makes them subjects of His own kingdom. They become obedient, useful, and serviceable to Him; therefore, He is more than a conqueror. Converted sinners not only lay down their weapons and fight no more against Christ, but join Him in His camp and fight *for* Christ. Now they use their reason for Christ and not against Him. Some said of Jerome, Origen, and Tertullian that they came into Canaan laden with Egyptian gold: they came into the Church full of excellent learning and abilities with which they eminently served Jesus Christ. "Oh blessed victory where the conqueror, and conquered, both triumph together!" And thus enemies and rebels are subdued, and made subjects of the spiritual kingdom of Christ. Hence, we affirm the doctrine that *Jesus Christ exercises a kingly power over the souls of all whom the gospel subdues to His obedience.*

No sooner were the Colossians delivered out of the power of darkness than they were *immediately* translated into the kingdom of Christ, the dear Son: "Who hath delivered us from the power of darkness, and hath translated us into the kingdom of his dear Son" (Colossians 1:13). This kingdom of Christ, which is our present subject, is the internal spiritual kingdom which is within the saints. Jesus said, "The kingdom of God is within you" (Luke 17:20, 21). Christ sits as an enthroned King in the hearts, consciences, and affections of His willing people: "Thy people shall be willing in the day of thy power, in the beauties of holiness" (Psalm 110:3). And His kingdom consists in "righteousness, peace, and joy in the Holy Ghost" (Romans 14:7). His internal government is properly a monarchy, and it must be so, for the right of governing people's consciences belongs to no one but Christ, who is both infinitely wise and most powerful.

How Sinners Are Converted

Doctrinally, we must understand how Christ obtains the throne in the hearts of people; how He rules in their hearts, and by what acts He exercises His kingly authority; and the privileges of those souls over whom He reigns.

We must not only understand these things, but also apply them to our lives. We will open up these doctrines and apply them in the following pages.

First, *How does Christ obtain the throne in the hearts of people.* The house is conveyed to Christ by the one who built it, but the strong man keeps armed possession of it till a stronger one than he comes and ejects him (see Luke 9:20–22). Christ must fight His way into the soul, though He has a right to enter as it is His dearly purchased possession. So He fights. For when the time of redemption is come, He sends forth His armies to subdue His enemies. The Lord Jesus has armies of prophets, apostles, evangelists, pastors, and teachers under the conduct of His Spirit. They are armed with the two-edged sword, the Word of God, which is sharp and powerful (Hebrews 4:12). But that is not all. He causes armies of convictions and spiritual troubles to surround and pinch His enemies on every side, so that they know not what to do. Like a shower of arrows, these convictions strike—point-blank—into their consciences; as Luke reported: "When they heard this, they were pricked to the heart, and said, Men and brethren, what shall we do?" (Acts 2:37). Christ's arrows are sharp in the hearts of His enemies, whereby they fall under Him (see Psalm 14:5, 6). By these convictions, He batters down all their loose, vain hopes and levels them with the earth.

Now, from the general mercy of God, the example of others, etc., all their weak pleas and defenses prove to be as paper walls to them. These shake their hearts, even to the very foundation, and overturn every high thought that exalts itself against the Lord. This day, in which Christ sits down before the soul, and summons it by such messengers as these, is a day of distress within. Yes, there is no day of trouble like this one. But even though it is so, Satan has so deeply entrenched himself in the mind and will that the soul yields not at the first summons until its armaments within are spent, and all its towers of pride and walls of vain confidence are undermined by the gospel and shaken down about its ears. Then the soul desires a peace treaty with Christ. Oh how the soul would be glad of terms, any terms, if it may but save its life. Now the soul sends many such messengers as these to Christ, who is come now to the very gates of the soul: "Mercy, Lord, mercy. Oh, if I were assured You would receive, spare, and pardon me, I would open to You the next moment!" Now the merciful King, whose only design is to conquer the heart, hangs forth the white flag of mercy before the soul, giving it hope that it shall be spared, pitied, and pardoned if it yields itself to Christ, even though it has long been in rebellion against Him. There are at the council-table of a person's own heart at this time many staggerings, hesitations, irresolutions, doubts, fears, scruples, half-resolves, and reasonings for and against yielding. Sometimes there is no hope, and the soul argues, "Christ will slay me if I go forth to Him," and then it trembles and says, "But then, who ever found Him that way that has tried Him? Other souls have yielded and found mercy beyond all their expectations. I have been a desperate enemy against Him, but I will admit my rebellion. I have the word of a King for it: 'Let the wicked forsake his way, and the unrighteous man his thoughts; and let him turn to the Lord, and he will have mercy on him; and to our God, for he will abundantly pardon him' " (Isaiah 55:7).

A thousand such debates the soul will have as it considers

that if it abides in rebellion it must perish. And then it will be encouraged by the messages of grace; such as, "Wherefore he is able to save to the uttermost, all that come unto God by him," and "He that cometh to me, I will in nowise cast out," and "Come unto me all ye that labor, and are heavy laden, and I will give you rest" (Hebrews 7:25; John 6:37; Matthew 11:28). The soul at last resolves to open to Christ, and says, "Stand open ye everlasting gates, and be ye opened ye everlasting doors, and the King of glory shall come in." Now, the will spontaneously opens to Christ: that royal fort submits and yields; all the affections open to Him. The will brings Christ the keys of all the rooms in the soul. Concerning the triumphant entrance of Christ into the soul, we may say, as the Psalmist rhetorically speaks concerning the triumphant entrance of Israel into Canaan: "The mountains skipped like rams, and the little hills like lambs; what aileth thee, O thou sea, that thou fleddest? Thou Jordan, that thou wast driven back?" (Psalm 114:5–6). So here, in rhetorical triumph, we may say, the mountains and the hills skipped like rams, and the fixed and obstinate will starts from its own basis and center; the rocky heart breaks in two. A poor soul comes into the Word of God full of ignorance, pride, self-centeredness, desperate hardness, and fixed resolutions to go on in its own way; and, by an hour's debate, the tide turns, the Jordan is driven back. The hard heart relents and the waters gush out; thus the soul is won to Christ. The soul thus comes in to Christ by free and hearty submission, desiring nothing more than to come under the government of Christ for the time to come.

How Christ Rules the Converted

There are six things in which Christ exerts His kingly authority over the converted.

1. He imposes a new law upon them, and enjoins them to be exacting and punctual in their obedience to it. It is proper for Christ, who rules absolutely and monarchically over the souls of and consciences of people, to bind them by His own authority. None but Christ can do it, because the authority of Christ is infinite and the authority of a husband cannot be given to any other. Before conversion the soul could endure no restraint. Its lusts gave it laws: "We ourselves were sometimes foolish, disobedient, serving divers lusts and pleasures" (Titus 3:3). Whatever the flesh craved and the sensual appetite whined after, it must have, no matter what the cost. If damnation were the price of it, the flesh would have it, provided it should not be paid at present. After conversion, the soul will not be any longer without the law of God, but under the law of Christ. Those are the articles of peace to which the soul willingly subscribes in the day of its admission to mercy. The converted sinner willingly obeys Jesus at the command, "Take my yoke upon you, and learn of me" (Matthew 11:29). This "law of the spirit of life which is in Christ Jesus makes them free from the law of sin and death" (Romans 8:2). Here is much strictness, but no bondage; for the law is not only written in Christ's statute book, the Bible, but copied out by His Spirit upon the hearts of His subjects in correspondent principles which makes obedience a pleasure and self-denial easy. Christ's yoke is lined with love, so that it never galls the necks of His people: "His commandments are not grievous" (1 John 5:3). The soul that comes under Christ's government must receive law from Christ; and under law every thought of the heart must come.

2. He rebukes and chastises souls for the violations and transgressions of His law. That is another act of Christ's regal authority: "whom he loves he rebukes and chastens" (Hebrews 12:6-7). These chastisements of Christ are either by the rod of *providence* upon their bodies, and outward com-

forts, or upon their spirits and inward comforts. Sometimes His rebukes are smart upon the outward man, "for this cause, many among you are weakly and sick, and many sleep" (1 Corinthians 11:30). They had not that due regard to His body that became them, and He will make their bodies to smart for it. And He had rather their flesh should smart, than their souls should perish. Sometimes He spares their outward man, and afflicts the inner man, which is a much smarter rod. He withdraws peace, and takes away joy from the spirits of His people. The hidings of His face are sore rebukes. However, all is for emendation, not for destruction. And it is a great privilege of Christ's subjects to have an occasional and sanctified rod to keep them from the ways of sin: "Thy rod and thy staff, they comfort me" (Psalm 23:3). Others are allowed to go on stubbornly in the way of their own hearts. Christ will not spend a rod upon them for their good, will not call them to account for any of their transgressions, but will reckon with them for all together in hell.

3. Another regal act of Christ is the restraining and keeping back His servants from iniquity, and withholding them from those courses which their own hearts would incline and lead them to; for, even in them there is a spirit bent toward backsliding, but the Lord in tenderness over them, keeps back their souls from iniquity, even when they are upon the very brink of sin: "My feet were almost gone, my steps were well nigh slipt" (Psalm 73:2). Then the Lord prevents sin by removing the occasion providentially, or by helping them to resist the temptation, graciously assisting their spirits in the trial, so that no temptation shall befall them, but a way of escape shall be opened, that they may be able to bear it (see 1 Corinthians 10:13). And thus His people have frequent occasions to bless His name for His preventing goodness, when they are almost in the midst of all evil. And this I take to be the meaning of Galatians 5:16: "This, I say then, walk in the

Spirit, and ye shall not fulfill the lusts of the flesh"; you may be tempted by them, but you shall not fulfill them. The Spirit of God will cause the temptation to die, and wither away in the womb, in the embryo stage, so that it shall not come to a full birth.

4. He protects them in His ways, and does not allow them to relapse from Him into a state of sin and bondage to Satan anymore. Indeed, Satan is restless in His endeavors to reduce them to his obedience again. He never quits tempting and soliciting for their return. And where he finds a false professing Christian, he prevails. However, Christ keeps His own so they do not depart again. He prayed, thanking His Father, "All that thou hast given me I have kept, and none of them is lost, but the son of perdition" (John 17:12). They are "kept by the mighty power of God, through faith unto salvation" (1 Peter 1:5). Kept, as in a garrison, according to the importance of His Word. None are more safe than the people of God. They are "preserved in Christ Jesus" (Jude 1). It is not their own grace that secures them, but Christ's care, and continual watchfulness: "Our own graces left to themselves would quickly prove but weights, sinking us to our own ruin," as one speaks. This is God's covenant with His people: "I will put my fear in their hearts, that they shall not depart from me" (Jeremiah 32:4). Thus, as their King, He preserves them.

5. As a King, He rewards their obedience, and encourages their sincere service. Though all they do for Christ is duty, yet He has united their comfort with their duty: "this I had, because I kept thy precepts" (Psalm 119:56). They are engaged to take this encouragement with them to every duty that He whom they seek "is a bountiful rewarder of such as diligently seek him" (Hebrews 11:6). Oh what a good master do the saints serve! Hear how a King expostulates with His subjects: "Have I been a barren wilderness, or a land of dark-

71

ness to you?" (Jeremiah 2:31). In other words, "Have I been such a hard master to you? Have you any reason to complain of my service? To whom have I been selfish, surely I have not been so to you. You have not found the ways or wages of sin like mine."

6. He pacifies all inward troubles and commands peace when their spirits are tumultuous. This "peace of God rules in their hearts" (Colossians 3:15). Christ acts the part of an umpire in appeasing strife within. When the tumultuous affections are up, and in a hurry; when anger, hatred, and revenge begin to rise in the soul, Christ hushes and stills all. "I will hearken [says the Church] to what God the Lord will speak, for he will speak peace to his people, and to his saints" (Psalm 75:8). He who said to the raging sea, "be still" and it obeyed Him; only He can pacify the disquieted spirit. They say of frogs that if they are croaking a lot in the night, then bring a light among them, and they will be quiet. Such a light is the peace of God among our disordered affections. These are Christ's regal acts. And He puts them forth upon the souls of His people, powerfully, sweetly, and suitably.

He puts forth His acts powerfully when He restrains us from sin, or impels us to duty. He does so with a soul determining efficacy, for "his kingdom is not in word, but in power" (1 Corinthians 4:20). Those whom His Spirit leads go empowered in the spirit to fulfill and discharge their duties. And yet, He does not rule by compulsion but most sweetly. His law is a law of love, written upon their hearts. The church is the Lamb's wife: "a bruised reed he shall not break, and smoking flax he shall not quench" (Isaiah 42:2–3). The Apostle Paul wrote: "I beseech you by the meekness and gentleness of Christ" (2 Corinthians 10:1). For God delights in *free*, not in *forced* obedience. He rules *children*, not *slaves*; and so His *Kingly power* is mixed with *fatherly love*. His yoke is not made of *iron*, but *gold*. He rules suitably to our natures, in a rational way: "I drew them with the cords of a man, with bands of love" (Hosea 11:4). He rules us in a way that is proper to convince our reason and work upon our ingenuity. And thus His eternal kingdom is administered by His Spirit, who is His vice-regent in our hearts.

The Privileges of the Converted

Third, we will look at the privileges pertaining to all the subjects of this spiritual kingdom. And they are such as follow.

1. These souls, over whom Christ reigns, are certainly and fully set free from the curse of the law. "If the Son makes you free, then are you free indeed" (John 8:36). I do not say they are free from obeying the law as a rule of life. Such a freedom is no privilege at all, but free from the rigorous exactions and terrible maledictions of it. To hear our liberty proclaimed from this bondage is the joyful sound indeed, the most blessed voice that ever our ears heard. And this all who are in Christ shall hear: "If we be led by the Spirit, we are not under the law" (Galatians 5:18). "Blessed are the people who hear this joyful sound" (Psalm 89:15).

2. Another privilege of Christ's subjects is freedom from the dominion of sin. "Sin shall not reign over them; for they are not under the law, but under grace" (Romans 6:14). One heaven cannot bear two suns; nor one soul two kings. When Christ takes the throne, sin quits it. It is true that the being of sin is still there, and its defiling and troubling power still remains; however, its dominion is abolished. Oh joyful tidings! Oh welcome day!

3. Another privilege of Christ's subjects is protection in all the troubles and dangers to which their souls or bodies are exposed. "This man shall be the peace, when the Assyrian shall come into our land, and when he shall tread in our

73

palaces" (Micah 5:5). Kings owe protection to their subjects. There is no one so able and so faithful in that work than Christ. All "thou gavest me, I have kept, and none is lost" (John 17:12).

4. Another privilege of Christ's subjects is a merciful and tender bearing of their burdens and infirmities. They have a meek and patient king: "Tell the daughters of Zion, thy king cometh meek and lowly" (Matthew 21:5). "Take my yoke, and learn of me, for I am meek and lowly" (Matthew 9:29). The meek Moses could not bear the provocations of the people, but Christ bears all (see Numbers 11:12). "He carries the lambs in his arms, and gently leads them that be with young" (Isaiah 42:11). He is one who can have compassion upon the ignorant and those who are out of the way.

5. Sweet peace and tranquillity of soul is the privilege of the subjects of this kingdom, for this kingdom "consisteth in peace, and joy in the Holy Ghost" (Romans 14:17). Until souls come under His sceptre, they shall never find peace: "Come unto me, ye that are weary, I will give you rest." Yet, do not mistakenly infer that they have peace at all times; no, they often break that peace by sin. But they have the root of peace, the groundwork and cause of peace. If they do not have peace, still they have that which can be converted into peace at any time. They also are in a state of peace: "Being justified by faith, we have peace with God" (Romans 5:11). This is a feast everyday, a mercy which only they can duly value who are in the depths of trouble for sin.

6. Everlasting salvation is the privilege of all over whom Christ reigns. Prince and Savior are joined together (see Acts 5:31). If you can say, "thou shalt guide me with thy counsels," then you can add what follows, "and afterwards bring me to glory" (Psalm 73:24). Indeed, the *kingdom of grace* does bring up children for the *kingdom of glory*. And to speak as the thing is, the kingdom of heaven has begun in the kingdom

of grace. The difference between the kingdoms is not specific, but only gradual; therefore, both kingdoms bear the name of the kingdom of heaven. The King is the same and the subjects are the same. The subjects of the kingdom of grace are shortly to be translated to that kingdom.

I have named indeed only a few of the inestimable privileges of Christ's subjects.

A Personal Application

How great is their sin and misery who continue in bondage to sin and Satan, and refuse the government of Christ! Who had rather sit under the shadow of that bramble, than under the sweet and powerful government of Christ. Satan writes his laws in the blood of his subjects, grinds them with cruel oppression, wears them out with bondage to different lusts, and rewards their service with everlasting misery. And yet how few are weary of it and willing to come over to Christ! Gurnal wrote in *The Christian Armor*, "Behold, Christ is in the field, sent of God to recover his right and your liberty. His royal standard is pitched in the gospel, and proclamation made, that if any poor sinners, weary of the Devil's government, and laden with the miserable chains of his spiritual bondage, (so as these irons of his sins enter into his very soul, to afflict it with the sense of them) shall thus come and repair to Christ, he shall have protection from God's justice, the Devil's wrath, and sin's dominion; in a word, he shall have rest, and that glorious."

Still, how few stir a foot toward Christ, but are willing to have their ears bored, marked as perpetual slaves to that cruel tyrant? Oh when will sinners be weary of their bondage, and sigh after deliverance! If any such poor soul shall read these lines, let them know, and I do proclaim it in the name of my royal Master, and give him the word of a King for it that he shall not be rejected by Christ (see John 6:37). Come, poor sinners, come; the Lord Jesus is a merciful King, and never did, nor ever will execute the poor repentant sinner who submits to His mercy.

Does it concern us to inquire and know whose government we are under, and who is king over our souls: whether Christ or Satan be on the throne and sways the sceptre over our souls? The work I would now engage your soul in is the same that Jesus Christ will thoroughly and effectually do in the great day of judgment. Then will He gather out of His kingdom everything that offends, separate the tares and wheat, divide the whole world into two ranks or grand divisions, no matter how many divisions and subdivisions there are now. It concerns you to know who is Lord and King in your soul. To help you in this great work, make use of the following hints.

Oh how many of us would have Jesus Christ divided into halves that we might take the half of Him only; His office, Savior, and salvation? But *Lord* is a cumbersome word, and to obey, and work out our own salvation, and perfect holiness is the cumbersome and stormy north side of Christ that we shift off. "To whom do you yield your obedience? His subjects and servants ye are to whom ye obey" (Romans 6:16). It is only a mockery to give Jesus Christ the empty titles of Lord and King, while you give your real service to sin and Satan. "Then are ye his disciples, if ye do whatsoever he commands you" (John 15:14). He that is Christ's servant in jest shall be damned in earnest. Christ does not compliment with you: His pardons, promises, and salvation are real. Oh let your obedience be real too! Let it be sincere and universal obedience; this will be evidence of your unfeigned subjection to Christ. Do not dare to do anything until you know Christ's pleasure and will (see Romans 12:2). Enquire of Christ, as David did of the Lord (see 1

Samuel 23:9–11). Ask, "Lord may I do this or that? Or shall I not do this? I beseech You to tell me."

Have you the power of godliness or a form of it only? There are many who only trifle in religion, and play about the skirts and borders of it. They spend their time in barren controversies. But they do not concern themselves with the power of Christian faith and the life of godliness, which consists in communion with God in duties and ordinances, which promotes holiness and mortifies their lusts. But surely, "the kingdom of God is not in word, but in power" (1 Corinthians 4:20). It is not meat and drink or dry disputes about meat and drink, but "righteousness and peace, and joy in the Holy Ghost"; for the one that "in these things serveth Christ, is acceptable to God, and approved of men" (Romans 14:17–18). Oh, I am afraid when the great host of professing Christians shall be tried by these rules, they will shrink up into a little handful, as Gideon's host did.

Have you the special saving knowledge of Christ? All His subjects are translated out of the kingdom of darkness (see Colossians 1:13). The devil that ruled over you in the days of your ignorance is called *the ruler of the darkness of this world*. His subjects are all blind, else he could never rule them. As soon as their eyes are open, they run out of his kingdom, and there is no retaining them in subjection to him any longer. Inquire then whether you are brought out of darkness into this marvelous light! Do you see your condition, how sad, miserable, wretched your sinful condition is? Do you see your remedy: only in Christ and His precious blood? Do you see the true way of obtaining interest in that blood: by faith alone? Does this knowledge run into practice, and make you lament heartily your misery by sin? Do you thirst after Christ and His righteousness? Do you strive continually for a heart to believe and close with Christ? This will be evidence for you as to whether you are translated out of the kingdom of darkness into the kingdom of Christ.

With whom do you delightfully associate yourself? Who are your chosen companions? You may see to whom you belong by the company you join yourself to. What do the subjects of Christ have to do among the slaves of Satan? If the subjects of one kingdom are in another king's dominion, they love to be together with their own countrymen, rather than the natives of the place; so do the servants of Christ. They are a company of themselves, as it is said, "They went to their own company" (Acts 4:23). I know the subjects of both kingdoms are here mingled, and we cannot avoid the company of sinners except we go out of the world, but yet all your delights should be with the saints and in the excellent things of the earth (see 1 Corinthians 5:10; Psalm 16:3).

Do you live holy and righteous lives? If not, you may claim interest in Christ as your King, but He will never acknowledge your claim. "The sceptre of his kingdom is a sceptre of righteousness" (Psalm 45:6). If you oppress, go beyond, and cheat your brethren, and yet call yourself Christ's subject, what greater reproach can you study to cast upon Him? What is Christ, the King of cheats? Does He patronize such things as these? No, no, fall into your own place. You belong to another prince, and not to Christ.

Does Christ exercise such a kingly power over the souls of all those who are subdued by the gospel to Him? Oh then let all who are under Christ's government walk as the subjects of such a King. Let the whole world follow the example of the Prince. Imitate your King: the examples of kings are very influential upon their subjects. Your King has commanded you not only to take His yoke upon you, but also to learn of Him. "If any man say that he is Christ's, let him walk even as Christ walked" (1 John 2:6). Your King is meek and patient, as a lamb for meekness: shall His subjects be lions for fierceness? Your King was humble and lowly, will you be proud and lofty? Does this become the kingdom of Christ? Your King was a self-denying King. He could deny His outward comforts, ease, honor, and life; giving up all to serve His Father's design and accomplish your salvation. Shall His servants be self-centered and self-seeking people, who will expose His honor and hazard their own souls for the trifles of time? God forbid. Your King fulfilled His work on earth in pain, labor, and diligence. Let not His servants be lazy and slothful. Oh imitate your King, follow the pattern of your King. This will give you comfort now and boldness in the day of judgment, if you live in the world as He did (see 1 John 4:17).

5
Providential Blessings

*I*n a thankful and humble adoration of the grace of God in bringing the Ephesians to believe in Christ, the Apostle Paul wrote to them: "And hath put all things under his feet, and gave him to be the head over all things to the church" (Ephesians 1:22). The effect of God's power that raised their hearts to believe in Christ is compared with that other glorious effect of it, even the raising of Christ from the dead. God's power raised Christ from a low estate, even from the dead, to a very high and glorious state, to be the head both of the *world* and of the *church*. Christ is the head of the world by way of dominion. He is the head of the church by way of union and special influence. He rules the world for the good of His people in it. "He gave him to be the head over all things to the church."

The Dominion of Christ

In the above scripture, seriously consider these four things.

First, consider the dignity and authority committed to Christ: "He hath put all things under his feet." There is full, ample, and absolute dominion in Christ. Those over whom He reigns are in subjection to Him. His Father delegated this power to Him: for besides the essential, native, ingenious power and dominion over all which Christ has as God, and is common to every Person in the Godhead, there is a mediatory dispensed authority which is proper to Him as Mediator, which He receives as the reward or fruit of His suffering.

Second, Christ alone receives this authority, power, and dominion. Whatever authority and power any creature has is derived from God, whether it is political or ecclesiastical. Jesus Christ is the only Lord. He is the fountain of all power.

Third, the object of Christ's dominion, of His authority, is the whole creation, *all things are put under his feet.* He rules from sea to sea, even to the utmost bounds of God's creation: "Thou hast given him power over all flesh" (John 17:2). All creatures, rational and irrational, angels, devils, men, winds, seas, obey Him.

Fourth, the design for which Christ governs and rules His universal empire is for the church. He obtains His dominion for the good of the church, for the advantage, comfort, and salvation of the chosen remnant for which He died. He purchased the Church, and God the Father put all things into His hand to order and dispose as He pleases, so that He might have the highest assurance that His blood should not be wasted.

We must never forget, but always remind ourselves of this doctrine: *All the affairs of the kingdom of providence are ordered and determined by Jesus Christ for the special advantage and everlasting good of His redeemed people.* "As thou hast given him power over all flesh, that he should give eternal life to as many as thou hast given him," so "all things work together for good to them that love God, to them that are called according to his purpose" (John 17:2; Romans 8:28).

Jesus Christ has a providential influence upon all the affairs of this world, and we know this from scriptural assertions and rational observations made upon the actings of things here below. The first chapter of Ezekiel contains an admirable scheme of providence. There you see how all the wheels are guided by the Spirit that is in them, and in verse twenty-six, the supreme cause is one like the Son of man, which is the preincarnate Jesus Christ sitting upon the throne and giving forth orders for the government of all. The wheels are like the motions and revolutions here on earth, which are guided by the Spirit. If this is not so, then why are there such strong combinations and predispositions of people and things to such ends and issues without any communications or councils among them, as in Israel's deliverance from Egypt, and innumerable other instances? Certainly, if ten people from several places should all meet at one place about one business, without any prior appointment among themselves, it would be an argument that their motions were secretly overruled by some invisible agent. How is it that such marvelous effects are produced in the world by causes that carry no proportion to them? In a word, if Christ has no providential influence, how are His people in all ages preserved in the midst of so many millions of potent and malicious enemies, among whom they live as sheep in the midst of wolves? How can a bush burn and not be consumed, apart from God's providence? But my business is not to prove that there is a Providence, which none but atheists deny. I shall show by what acts Jesus Christ administers this kingdom, and in what manner.

Christ Rules the Kingdom of Providence

He rules and orders the kingdom of Providence by *supporting, permitting, restraining, limiting, protecting, punishing, and rewarding* those over whom He reigns providentially.

He *supports* the world and all creatures in it by His power. He said, "My Father works hitherto, and I work" (John 5:17). And Paul wrote, "in him [that is, in Christ] all things consist" (Colossians 1:17). It is a considerable part of Christ's glory to have a whole world of creatures owing their being and hourly conservations to Him. The parts of the world are not coupled and fastened together as the parts of a house, whose beams are pinned and nailed to each other; but rather as several rings of iron, which hang together by the power of a magnet. This world would have been destroyed to the foundation when sin entered if Christ had not stepped in to shore up the reeling planet. For the sake of His redeemed who inhabit the world, He does and will prop up the world by His omnipotent power. And when He has gathered all His elect out of it into the kingdom above, then will He set fire to the four quarters of it, and it shall lie in ashes. Meanwhile, He is "given for a covenant to the people, to establish the earth" (Isaiah 49:8).

He *permits* and allows the worst of creatures in His dominion to be and act as they do. "The deceived, and the deceiver are his" (Job 12:16). Even those who fight against Christ and His people receive both power and permission from Him. Do not say that it is unworthy of the most Holy God to permit such evils which He could prevent if He pleased. For as He permits no more than He will overrule to His praise, so His very permission is holy and just. Christ's working is not to be confused with the creature's. Pure sunbeams are not tainted by the noisome vapors of the dunghill on which they shine. His holiness has no fellowship with iniquity, nor are the transgressions of men at all excused by His allowing them to occur. "He is a rock, his work is perfect, but they have corrupted themselves" (Deuteronomy 32:4–5). This holy permission is but the withholding of those restraints from their lusts, and denying those common assistances which He is no way bound to give them. The Scripture says, "He suffered all nations to walk in their own ways" (Acts 14:16). And yet should He permit sinful creatures to act out all the wickedness that is in their hearts, there would neither remain peace nor order in the world.

He powerfully *restrains* creatures by the bridle of Providence from the commission of those things to which their hearts are committed. The psalmist declared, "The remainder of wrath thou will restrain." He lets forth just so much as shall serve His holy ends and no more. And truly this is one of the glorious mysteries of Providence which amazes the serious and considerate person, to see the spirit of a creature fully set to do mischief, powerful enough to carry it out and a door of opportunity standing open for it, and yet, the effect strangely hindered. The strong propensities of the will are inwardly checked, as in the case of Laban or as in the case of Sennacherib, a diversion is strangely cast in their way so that their hands cannot perform their intention (see Genesis 31:24; 2 Kings 19:7-8). Julian had two great designs before him; one was to conquer the Persians and the other was to root out the Galileans—as he, by way of contempt, called the Christians. But he began with the Persians, intending to make a sacrifice of all the Christians to his idols. He perished at the first attempt. Oh the wisdom of Providence!

Jesus Christ *limits* the creatures in their acting, assigning them their boundaries and lines of liberty to which they may go, but beyond which they may not go. "Fear none of these things that ye shall suffer; behold, the devil shall cast some of you into prison and ye shall have tribulation ten days" (Revelation 2:10). They would have cast them into their graves, but it shall only be into prison. They would have stretched out their hands upon all, but only some would be exposed. They would have kept them there perpetually, but it would be for a limited time. They went as far as they had power to go, not as far as they willed to go. Four hundred and thirty years of servitude were determined upon the people of God in Egypt; and then, *even in that very night*, God brought them forth. For then, "the time of the promise was come" (Acts 7:17).

The Lord Jesus providentially *protects* His people amidst a world of enemies and dangers. Christ appeared unto Moses in the flaming bush, and preserved it from being consumed. The bush signified the people of God in Egypt. The fire flaming on it symbolized the exquisite sufferings they endured, the safety of the bush amidst the flames, the Lord's admirable care and protection of His poor suffering ones. No one is so tenderly careful as Christ.

He *punishes* the evildoers and repays by Providence the mischiefs they do, or intend to do. Pharaoh, Sennacherib, both the Julians, and innumerable others, are the lasting monuments of His righteous retribution. It is true, a sinner may do evil one hundred times, and his days be prolonged; but often God hangs some eminent sinners in chains, as spectacles and warnings to others. Many a heavy blow hath Providence given to the enemies of God from which they were never able to recover. Christ rules with a rod of iron in the midst of His enemies (see Psalm 110:2).

He *rewards* by Providence the services done to Him and to His people. Out of this treasure of Providence God repays often those who serve Him, giving a hundred-fold reward now in this life (see Matthew 19:29). His active, vigilant Providence is working in all the needs, difficulties, and troubles of His creatures; but especially upon such as Christianity brings us into. The people of God could write huge volumes of experiences upon this subject. What a pleasant history would it be to read the strange, constant, wonderful, and unexpected actings of Providence, for those who have left themselves in His care.

How Christ Rules Providence

We shall enquire into how Jesus Christ administers His providential kingdom. The means or instruments He uses in governing the providential kingdom are either angels or humans: "the angels are ministering creatures, sent forth by him for the good of them that shall be heirs of salvation" (Hebrews 1:14). The angels of God have dear and tender love and respect for the saints. To them, God, as it were, puts forth His children to nurse, and they are tenderly careful of them while they live, and bring them home in their arms to their Father when they die. And as angels, so humans are the servants of Providence; yes, bad men as well as good. On that account, Cyrus is called "God's servant." Evil men fulfill God's will while they are prosecuting their own lusts. But good men delight to serve Providence. They and the angels are fellow-servants in one house, and to one master. Yes, there is not a creature in heaven, earth, or hell that Jesus Christ cannot providentially use to serve His good ends, through whom He can promote His designs. But whatever the instrument is, Christ's use of it is holy, judicious, sovereign, profound, irresistible, harmonious, and to the saints unique.

Jesus Christ is holy, and His providential work is holy too. Though He permits, limits, orders, and overrules many unholy people and actions, He still works like himself, most holy and pure throughout. "The Lord is righteous in all his ways, and holy in all his works" (Psalm 145:17). It is easier to separate light from a sunbeam than holiness from the work of Jesus Christ. The best of people cannot escape their fallen nature in their most holy actions, but no evil cleaves to God.

Christ's providential working is not only most pure and

holy, but also most wise and judicious. His actions are not made in blindness to circumstances, but in deep counsel and wisdom. The wisdom of Providence manifests itself principally in the choice of circumstances for the people of God that shall most effectually promote their eternal happiness. And herein things go quite beyond our human understanding and comprehension. Human reason thinks God's medicine is a destructive poison, when He means it for our comfort and good. One has said that in heaven the blessed shall see in God all things and circumstances that pertained to them were excellently accommodated for saving their souls even though they seemed to be at cross purposes with their desires. The most wise Providence looks beyond us. Providence looks to the end and suits things to the end, and not to our temporal fond desires.

The providence of Christ is most supreme and sovereign: "Whatsoever he pleaseth, that he doth in heaven and in earth, and in all places" (Psalm 135:6). "He is Lord of lords, and King of kings" (Revelation 19:16). The greatest monarchs on earth are but little bits of clay; and just as the worms, they depend on Him: "By me kings reign, and princes decree justice; by me princes rule, nobles, even all the judges of the earth" (Proverbs 8:15–16).

Providence is profound and inscrutable. The judgments of Christ are "a great deep, and his footsteps are not known" (Psalm 36:6). There are hard texts in the *works* as well as in the *words* of Christ. The wisest heads have been at a loss in interpreting some providences (see Jeremiah 12:1–2; Job 21:7). The angels can have the hands of a man under their wings, they work secretly and mysteriously (see Ezekiel 1:8).

Providence is irresistible in its designs and motions, for all providences are merely fulfillments and accomplishments of God's immutable decrees: "He works all things according to his own will" (Ephesians 1:11). Hence, the instruments whereby God executes His wrath are called "chariots coming between two mountains of brass" (see Zechariah 6:1). When the Jews put Christ to death, they did what "the hand and counsel of God had before determined to be done" (Acts 4:28). No one can resist or oppose the providence of God: "I will work, and who shall let it?" (Isaiah 43:13).

The providences of Christ are harmonious. There are secret chains, and invisible connections between the works of Christ. We do not know how to reconcile promises and providences together, nor yet providences one with another; but certainly they all *work together* (see Romans 8:28). Jesus does not do and then undo. He does not destroy one providence by another. Just as the seasons of the year work together to produce the harvest, so do the providences of God.

The providences of Christ work in a special and peculiar way for the good of the saints. His providential work in this world is subordinated to His spiritual kingdom. "He is the Savior of all men, especially of them that believe" (1 Timothy 4:1). Only those who are saved have the blessings of Providence. Things are so laid and ordered that their eternal good is promoted and secured by all that Christ does.

Christ's Providential Rule Encourages Us

Remember the one to whom you are indebted for your lives, liberties, comforts, and all that you enjoy in this world. Jesus Christ orders all for you. He is, indeed, in heaven, out of your sight; however, though you do not see Him, He sees you and takes care of all your concerns. When someone told Silentiarus of a plot laid to take away his life, he answered, "If God take no care of me, how do I live? How have I escaped until now?" Scripture says, "In all thy ways acknowledge him" (Proverbs 3:6). Jesus Christ does all for you that is done. He looks down from heaven upon all those who fear Him. He sees when you are in danger by temptation, and He casts in a providence, you do not know how, to save you. He sees when you are sad, and orders reviving providences to refresh you. He sees when corruptions prevail, and orders humbling providences to purge them. Whatever mercies you have received to this point in your life are the orderings of Christ for you. And you should carefully observe how the promises and providences have kept equal pace with one another, and both have gone step by step with you even to this day.

God has left the government of the whole world in the hands of Christ, and trusted Him over all. Leave all your concerns in the hands of Jesus Christ too, and know that the infinite wisdom and love which rules the world manages everything that relates to you. Your concerns are in good hands, and infinitely better than if they were in your own. I remember when Melanchton was under some despondencies of spirit about the estate of God's people in Germany, and Luther chided him for it: "Let Philip cease to rule the world." It is none of our work to steer the course of providence or direct its motions, but to submit quietly to the one who does. There is an itch in the best of people to dispute with God: Jeremiah said, "Let me talk with thee of thy judgment" (Jeremiah 12:1–2). Yes, how apt we are to regret some providences, as if they did not promote at all the glory of God or our own good. We are prone to limit providence to our way and time. Thus the "Israelites tempted God, and limited the holy One" (Psalm 78:18, 41). How often do we unbelievingly distrust providence as though it could never accomplish what we profess to expect and believe? The Jews declared, "Our bones are dry, our hope is lost; we are cut off for our part" (Ezekiel 37:11). There are only a few Abrahams among believers, who "against hope, believed in hope, giving glory to God" (Romans 4:20). And it is but too common for good people to repine and fret at providence, when their wills, lusts, or desires are crossed by providence: this was the great sin of Jonah. Brethren, these things ought not to be so. Did you seriously consider, either the design or providence, which is to bring about the gracious designs and purposes of God upon you, which were laid before this world was created? Have you considered that it is lifting up your wisdom against His, as if you could better order your affairs, if you only had the conduct and management of them? Don't you know that you are in the hands of a great and dreadful God, and you are as clay in a potter's hands, that He may do what He will with you and all that is yours without giving you an account of any of His matters (see Job 33)? Has not providence cast down others, who are as good by nature as you are, from the top of health, wealth, honors, and pleasures, to the bottom of hell? If you would consider how often providence has formerly baffled and befooled you, then you would retract with shame your rash, headlong censures of providence and confess your folly and ignorance. If such considerations could have a place with you in your troubles and temptations, they would quickly mold your heart into a better and more quiet frame.

Oh that I could but persuade you to resign all to Jesus Christ. He is a wise workman, and has the power to do as He pleases. Keep this as a good rule: *"Let God work out all that He intends, but have patience until He has put the last hand to His work, and then find fault with it, if you can."* You have heard of the patience of Job; now wait until you have seen "the end of the Lord" (James 5:11).

Since Jesus Christ is Lord and King over the providential kingdom, and that for the good of His people, let no one who is Christ's stand in a slavish fear of any creature. Grotius put down a good note when he wrote, "It is a marvelous consolation that Christ has so great an empire, and that He governs it for the good of His people, as a head consulting the good of the body." Our head and husband is the Lord-general of all the hosts of heaven and earth. No creature can move hand or tongue without His permission or order. The power they have is given to them from above. The serious consideration of this truth will make the feeblest spirit cease trembling, and set it to singing: "The Lord is king of all the earth, sing ye praises with understanding" (Psalm 47:7). Let everyone who has understanding take comfort in this truth. Has He not given you abundant security in many express promises, that all shall issue well for you who fear Him? God has promised, "It shall be well with them that fear God," even with them that fear before Him. The very understanding of our relation to such a King should, in itself, be sufficient security; for He is the universal, supreme, absolute, meek, merciful, victorious, and immortal King.

He sits in glory at the Father's right hand; and, to make His seat the easier, His enemies are a footstool for Him. His love to His people is unspeakably tender and fervent. He who touches His people, "touches the apple of his eye" (Zechariah 2). And it is hardly imaginable that Jesus Christ will sit still and allow His enemies to thrust out His "eyes." We should not fear the wrath of man: "He that fears a man that shall die, forgets the Lord his Maker" (Isaiah 51:12–13). Jesus Christ loves you too well to sign any order to your ultimate harm, and without His order or permission no one can touch you.

Since the government of the world is in the hands of Christ, our engaging and entitling of Jesus Christ to all our affairs and business is the true and ready way to their success and prosperity. If all depend upon His pleasure, then wisdom demands we take Him along with us to every action and business. It is no lost time that is spent in prayer, wherein we ask His permission and beg His presence with us. Take it for a clear truth that which is not prefaced with prayer will be followed with trouble. Jesus Christ can easily dash all your designs in a moment, even if they are at the very birth and point of execution. It is a proverb among the Papists, that Mass and meat hinder no one. The Muslims will pray five times a day, however urgent their business may be. Should you blush that you undertake many enterprises without God? I reckon business as good as done if we have gotten Christ's permission to do it and engaged His presence to accompany us.

See Christ's hand in everything that befalls you, whether good or evil. "The works of the Lord are great, sought out of all them that have pleasure therein" (Psalm 111:2). How much good might we get by observation of the good or evil that befalls throughout our life! In all the evils of trouble and afflictions that befall you, see Jesus Christ, and study these four things in afflictions.

1. Study His sovereignty and dominion; for He creates and forms afflictions. They do not rise out of the dust, nor do they befall you accidentally, but He raises them up and gives them their commission. He chooses the instrument of your trouble. He makes the rod afflictive as He pleases. He orders the continuance and end of your troubles. And they will not cease to be afflictive to you until Christ says, "Leave off, it is enough." The Centurion wisely considered this when he told Jesus, "I have soldiers under me, and I say to one, Go, and he goeth; to another, Come, and he cometh" meaning, that as his soldiers were at his beck and command, so diseases were at Christ's beck, to come and go as He ordered them.

2. Study the wisdom of Christ in the midst of your troubles. And His wisdom shines out many ways in them. It is evident in choosing such *kinds* of trouble for you. Christ allows this rather than that trouble because this one is more

apt to work upon and purge out the corruption that most predominates in you. In the *degrees* of your troubles, allowing them to work to such a height, else not reach their end, but no higher, lest they overwhelm you.

3. Study the tenderness and compassion of Christ over His afflicted. Oh think if the devil had but the mixing of my cup! How much more bitter would he make it! There would not be one drop of mercy; no, not of sparing mercy. In Christ, there is much mercy mixed with my troubles. There is mercy in this: that it is no worse. Am I afflicted? "It is of the Lord's mercy I am not consumed" (Lamentations 3:2). It might have been hell as well as this: there is mercy in His support of us in affliction. Others have, and I might have been left to sink and perish under my burdens. *Mercy* in deliverance out of affliction. Oh the tenderness of Christ over His afflicted!

4. Study the love of Christ to your soul in affliction. If He did not love you, He would not sanctify a rod to humble or reduce you, but let you alone to perish in your sin. "Whom I love, I rebuke and chasten" (Revelation 3:19). This is the device of love, to recover you to your God and prevent your ruin. Oh what an advantage would it be thus to study Christ in all your evils that befall you!

See and study Christ in all the good you receive from the hand of Providence. Turn both sides of your mercies, and view them in all their lovely circumstances. See them as suitable for you. How conveniently providence has ordered all things for you. You have a narrow heart, and a small estate suitable to it. If you had more of the world, it would be like a large sail to a little boat, which would quickly pull you under water. You have what is most suitable to you in all conditions.

See and study the seasonableness of your mercies, how they are timed to an hour. Providence brings forth all its fruits in due season. See also the peculiar nature of your mercies. Others have common mercies, but you have special mercies if you are a believer. Others have but a single enjoyment—the natural enjoyment of a matter—but you have a double sweetness in your enjoyments—the natural plus a spiritual joy in seeing the manner and the end goal of a matter.

Observe the order in which providence sends your mercies. See how one is linked strangely to another, and is the door to let in many. Sometimes one mercy is introductive to a thousand.

Lastly, observe the constancy of them, "they are new every morning" (Lamentations 3:23). How assiduously God visits your soul and body! Think, if there were a suspension of the care of Christ for one hour, that hour would be your ruin. Thousands of evils stand around you, watching when Christ will remove His eye from you, that they may rush in and devour you.

If we could study the providence of Christ our King in all the good and evil that befalls us in the world, then in every state we would be content (see Philippians 4:11). Then we should never be stopped, but furthered in our way by all that happens. Then would our experience swell to great volumes, which we might carry to heaven with us; and then should we answer all Christ's ends and purposes in every state He brings us into. Do this, and say, *"Thanks be to God for Jesus Christ."*

6

Heavenly Blessings

*C*hrist returned again to His Father. Having finished His whole work on earth, His Father called Him to sit down on the seat of honor and rest. This seat was prepared for Him at God's right hand, the place of honor. And all of His enemies are as a footstool under His feet, that makes it restful. How much the state and condition of Jesus Christ changed in just a few days! When He walked upon this earth, He groaned, wept, labored, suffered, sweat—yes, sweat blood—and found no rest in this world. But when He ascended into heaven, He entered into His rest. He is sitting forever in the highest and easiest throne prepared by the Father for Him when He had completed His work of redemption. Scripture says, "when he had by himself purged our sins, he sat down."

By His essential glory and dignity, Jesus Christ is the brightness of His Father's glory, the very splendor of glory. As the sun communicates its light and influences us by its beams, so God communicates His goodness and manifests himself by Christ. Jesus Christ is the express image of the character of God His Father. Not as the impressed image of a seal upon wax, but as the engraving in the seal itself. Thus

Christ is described by His essential glory.

The writer to the Hebrews also describes the work He wrought here on earth in His humbled state, and it was a glorious work, a work by His own single hand: "When he had by himself purged our sins." All the angels in heaven could not have done this work, but Christ did.

Lastly, the writer described the glory which was the reward of His work, a glory He now enjoys in heaven: "he sat down on the right hand of the Majesty on high." His Father clothed Him with the greatest power and highest honor that heaven itself could afford.

Christ Rules From God's Right Hand

Realizing that Jesus sat down on the right hand of the Majesty on high is transformingly glorious. Stephen had but a glimpse of Christ at His Father's right hand, and it caused "his face to shine, as it had been the face of an angel," (Acts 7:56). Christ's promotion was foretold and promised before His work of redemption: "The Lord said unto my Lord, sit thou at my right hand, until I make thine enemies thy footstool," (Psalm 110:1). And this promise was punctually fulfilled to Christ after His resurrection and ascension, when in His supreme exaltation He was seated far above all created beings in heaven and earth (see Ephesians 1:20–22).

The right hand is the hand of honor, the upper hand, where we place those whom we highly esteem and honor. King Solomon placed his mother at his right hand. So, in token of honor, God the Father set Christ at His right hand; which in our text is called the right hand of *Majesty*. The Majesty has, therefore, expressed more favor, delight, and honor to Jesus Christ than He ever did to any creature. "To which of the angels said he at any time, sit thou on my right hand?" (Hebrews 1:18).

The right hand is the hand of power. We call it the "weapon hand" and the "working hand." And the setting of Christ at the right hand shows the importance of His exaltation to the highest authority and most supreme dominion. Not that God the Father has taken himself out of authority, and advanced Christ above himself. No, "for in that he saith he hath put all things under him, it is manifest that he is excepted which did put all things under him" (1 Corinthians 15:27). To sit as an enthroned King at God's right hand imports power. Yes, the most sovereign and supreme power. And so, Christ himself calls the right hand at which He sits, "Hereafter ye shall see the Son of man sitting on the right hand of power" (Matthew 26:64).

Sitting at the right hand also signifies nearness in place, as we say, "at one's elbow." So this is applied to Christ in Psalm 110:5, "The Lord at thy right hand shall strike through kings in the day of his wrath." This means the Lord who is very near you, present with you, will subdue your enemies. This then is what we should understand by God's right hand: honor, power, and nearness.

What Sitting at God's Right Hand Implies

Let us see what is implied in Christ's sitting at God's right hand, with His enemies for His footstool. And if we attentively consider, we shall find that it implies many great and weighty things.

First, sitting at God's right hand implies the perfecting and completing of the work that He came into the world to do. After His work was ended, He sat down and rested from those labors. "Every priest standeth daily ministering, and offering oftentimes the same sacrifices: which can never take away sins: but this man when he had once offered one sacrifice for sins, for ever sat down on the right hand of God"

(Hebrews 10:11–12). Here God assigns a double difference between Christ and the Levitical priests. They stand, which is the posture of servants. Christ sits, which is the posture of a Lord. They stand daily, because their sacrifices cannot take away sin. Christ did His work fully, by one offering; and after that, sits or rests forever in heaven. The accurate and judicious Dr. Reynolds has observed that Christ's work was excellently illustrated for us in the Ark of the Covenant, which was a clear type of Jesus Christ, and particularly in this: the ark had rings by which it was carried up and down until at last it rested in Solomon's temple with glorious and triumphal solemnity (see also Psalm 132:8–9; 2 Chronicles 5:13). In the same way, Christ, while He was here on earth, being anointed with the Holy Spirit and wisdom, went about doing good, and having ceased from His works did at last enter into His rest, which is the heavenly temple (see Acts 10:38; Hebrews 5:10; and Revelation 11:19). They are said to sit down who rest from their labors and thereby refresh themselves. In this sense some understand Genesis 18:1 to speak of Christ. To sit at God's right hand in heaven is to rest in that eternal blessedness with God from these labors and miseries to which He voluntarily subjected himself for us.

Second, Christ sitting down at God's right hand denotes the high contentment and satisfaction of God His Father in Him and in His work. "The Lord said to my Lord, sit thou on my right-hand": the words are brought in as the words of the Father, welcoming Christ to heaven, congratulating the happy accomplishment of His most difficult work. It is as if He had said, "O my Son, what shall be done for You this day? You have finished a great work, and in all the parts of it You have acquitted yourself as an able and faithful servant to Me. What honors shall I now bestow upon You? The highest glory in heaven is not too high for You. Come sit at my right hand." Oh, how well is He pleased with Jesus Christ, and what He has done! He delighted greatly to behold Him here in His work on earth, and by a voice from heaven He told Him so, when He said, "Thou art my beloved Son, in whom I am well pleased" (2 Peter 1:17). Jesus told us, "Therefore doth my Father love me, because I lay down my life," for it was a work that God had set His heart upon from eternity. He took infinite delight in it.

Third, Christ's sitting down at God's right hand in heaven denotes the advancement of Christ's human nature to the highest honor, even to be the object of adoration of angels and humans. For it is properly His human nature that is the subject of all this honor and advancement. Being promoted to the right hand of Majesty is to become an object of worship and adoration. Not simply, as it is flesh and blood, but as it is personally united to the second person and enthroned in the supreme glory of heaven.

Here is the mystery, that flesh and blood should ever be advanced to the highest throne of majesty, and being there installed in that glory, we may now direct our worship to Him as *God-man*. To this end was His humanity so advanced that it might be adored and worshiped by all. "The Father hath committed all judgment to the Son, that all men should honor the Son, even as they honor the Father." And the Father will accept no honor which is not also Christ's honor. Therefore, it is added in the clause, "He that honoreth not the Son, honoreth not the Father which hath sent him" (John 5:22–23). Hence, the apostles, in the salutations of their letters, beg for grace, mercy and peace from God the Father and our Lord Jesus Christ; and in their valedictions, they pray for the grace of our Lord Jesus Christ for the churches.

Fourth, sitting at the right hand of God stresses the sovereignty and supremacy of Christ over all. The investiture of Christ with authority over the empire of both worlds belongs to Him who sits down upon His throne. When the Father said to Him, "Sit at my right hand," He did therein deliver to Him the dispensation and economy of the kingdom. This sitting down of Christ at the Father's right hand does not signify only that glory and essential kingdom which was common to the Son of God with the Father from eternity, for in this respect even the Holy Spirit sits at the right hand of God, but the economical and voluntary kingdom over which He is appointed as God-man and Mediator by the Father for the gathering in and defending of His church. The seat speaks of the awe-inspiring sceptre of government into His hand, and so the apostle interprets and understands it: "He must reign till he have put all his enemies under his feet" (1 Corinthians 15:25). And to this purpose, the same apostle accommodates (if not expounds) the words of the Psalmist, "Thou madest him a little lower than the angels," with respect to His humbled state on earth, "thou crownedst him with glory and honor, and didst set him over the works of thy hands, thou hast put all things in subjection under his feet" (Hebrews 2:7–8). He is absolute Lord over the spiritual kingdom and the Church (see Matthew 28:18–20). He is also Lord over the providential kingdom, the whole world (see Psalm 110:2). And this providential kingdom, being subordinate to His spiritual kingdom, He orders and rules this for the advantage and benefit of His kingdom (see Ephesians 1:22).

Fifth, to sit at God's right hand with His enemies for a footstool implies that Christ is the conqueror over all His enemies. To have His enemies under His feet denotes perfect conquest and complete victory. As when Joshua set his foot upon the necks of the kings. In a similar fashion, Tamerlane made proud Bajazet his footstool. Bajazet, who so often terrified the city of Constantinople, became as a dog and a footstool under Tamerlane. Sinners trampled Christ's name and His saints under their feet, and Christ will tread them under His feet. It is true indeed that this victory is incomplete and inconsumate; for now, "we see not yet all things put under him, but we see Jesus crowned with glory and honor," and that is enough. Enough to show the power of His enemies is now broken, and though they make some opposition, still it is to no purpose at all. For He is so infinitely above them that they must fall before Him. It is not with Christ as it was with Abijah, against whom Jeroboam prevailed, because he was young and tender-hearted, and could not withstand him. His incapacity and weakness gave the watchful enemy an advantage over him. I say, it is not so with Christ, He is at God's right hand. And all the power of God stands ready bent to strike through His enemies, as we read in Psalm 110:5.

Sixth, Christ's sitting in heaven denotes to us the great and wonderful change that is made upon the state and condition of Christ since His ascension into heaven. Ah, it is far otherwise with Him now than it was in the days of His humiliation here on earth. Oh, what a wonderful change has heaven made upon Him! It is good to compare in our thoughts the abasement of Christ and His exaltation together; as it were in columns, one over against the other. He was born in a stable, but now He reigns in His royal palace. Then He had a manger for His cradle, but now He sits on a chair of state. Then oxen and asses were His companions, now thousands of saints and ten thousands of angels minister round His throne. Then in contempt they called Him the "carpenter's son," now He has obtained a more excellent name than "angel." Then he was led away into the wilderness to be tempted by the devil, now it is proclaimed before Him, "let all the angels of God worship Him." Then He had no place to lay His head, now He is exalted to be the heir of all things. In His state of humiliation, He endured the insults of sinners; in His state of exaltation, He is adored and admired by saints and angels. Then "he had no form or comeliness; and when we saw him, there was no beauty, why we should desire him." Now, the beauty of His countenance shall send forth such glorious beams, as shall dazzle the eyes of all the celestial inhabitants round about Him. Oh what a change is this! Here He sweated, but there He sits. Here He groaned, but there He triumphs. Here He lay upon the ground, there He sits in the throne of glory. When He came to heaven, His Father did as it were thus speak to Him:

My dear Son, what a hard travail You have had. What a world of woe You have passed through in the strength of Your love to Me and the elect. You have been hungry, thirsty, weary, scourged, crucified, and reproached. Ah, what bad usage You have had in an ungrateful world! Not a day's rest for comfort since You went out from Me, but now Your suffering days are accomplished. Now Your rest is come, rest forevermore. Henceforth, sit at my right hand. Henceforth, You shall groan, weep, or bleed no more. Sit down at My right hand.

Seventh, Christ's sitting at God's right hand implies the advancement of believers to the highest honor. For this session of Christ's is for their sake, and there He sits as our representative, in which regard we are made to sit with Him in heavenly places, as the apostle says in Ephesians 2:6. How secure may we be who do now already possess the kingdom, meaning in our Head, Jesus Christ! This is all my hope, and all my confidence, namely, that we have a portion in that flesh and blood of Christ which is so exalted; therefore, where He reigns, we shall reign; where our flesh is glorified, we shall be glorified. Surely, it is a matter of exceeding joy to believe that Christ our Head, our flesh and blood, is in all this glory at His Father's right hand. *Thus we have opened the sense and importance of Christ's sitting at His Father's right hand.* Hence we infer the following.

Our Blessings From His Rule

If it is so great an honor to Christ to sit enthroned at God's right hand, what honor then is reserved in heaven for those who are faithful to Christ now in this earth? Christ prayed, and His prayer was heard: "That we may be with him to behold the glory that God hath given him" (John 17:24). What heart can conceive the felicity of such a sight? It made Stephen's face shine as the face of an angel, when he had but a glimpse of Christ at His Father's right hand.

But this is not all, though this be much, to be spectators of Christ in His throne of glory. We shall not only see Him in His throne, but also sit with Him enthroned in glory. To behold Him is much, but to sit with Him is more. I remember it was the saying of a heavenly Christian, now with Christ, "I would far rather look but through the hole of Christ's door, to see but one half of His fairest and most comely face (for He looks like heaven), supposing I should never win to see His excellency and glory to the full; than to enjoy the flower, the bloom, and chiefest excellency of the glory and riches of ten worlds." And you know how the Queen of the South fainted at the sight of Solomon in his glory. But this sight you shall have of Christ will change you into His likeness. The apostle said, "We shall be like him for we shall see him as he is" (1 John 3:2). He will place us, as it were, in His own throne with Him. So runs the promise in Revelation 3:21; "To him that overcometh, I will grant to sit with me in my throne; even as I also overcame, and am set down with my Father in his throne." The same is said in 2 Timothy 2:12; "If we suffer with him, we shall also reign with him." The Father set Christ on His right hand, and Christ will set the saints on His right hand; the sheep will be placed by the angels at the great day, and so the Church, under the figure of the daughter of Egypt, whom Solomon married, is placed "on the king's right hand, in gold of Ophir" (Psalm 15). This honor have all the saints.

These expressions indeed do not intend that the saints shall be set in higher glory than Christ; or that they shall have a parity of glory with Christ, for in all things He must have the pre-eminence. But they note the great honor that Christ will put upon the saints; as also, that His glory shall be their glory in heaven. "As the glory of the husband redounds to the wife"; and again, their glory will be His glory (see 2 Thessalonians 1:10). The glory will be a social glory. Oh, it is admirable to think that free grace has already mounted up poor dust and ashes.

To think how nearly related we are now to this royal, princely Jesus! But how much higher are the designs of grace, that are not yet come to their fullness, they look beyond all this that we now know! "Now are we the sons of God, but it doth not yet appear what we shall be" (1 John 3:2). Ah, what reason have you to honor Christ on earth, who is preparing such honors for you in heaven.

Since Christ Jesus is thus enthroned in heaven, then it is impossible that His interest should ever miscarry or sink on earth. The Church has many subtle and potent enemies. But as Haman could not prevail against the Jews while Esther their friend spoke for them to the king, no more can the enemies of the Church prevail while our Jesus sits at our Father's right hand. Will He allow His enemies, who are under His feet, to rise up and pull out His eyes? Surely those who touch His people touch the very apple of His eye (see Zechariah 2:8). And Paul wrote, "He must reign till his enemies are put under his feet" (1 Corinthians 15:25). The enemy under His feet shall not destroy the children in His arms. He sits in heaven on purpose to manage all to the advantage of His Church (see Ephesians 1:22). Are our enemies powerful? Lo, our King *sits on the right hand of power*. Are they subtle and deep in their contrivance? He who sits on the throne sees all they do. Heaven sees hell. "He that sits in heaven beholds," and derides their attempts (see Psalm 2:4). He may permit His enemies to trouble them in one place, but it shall be for their enlargement in another. For as with the sea, so it is with the Church: what it loses in one place, it gets in another; and so really loses nothing. Christ may allow us to be distressed outwardly, but we shall be recompensed with inward and better mercies; and so we shall lose nothing by that. A footstool you know is useful to him that treads on it, and serves to lift him up higher; so shall Christ's enemies be to Him and His own, though His enemies do not think in those terms now. What unique benefits the oppositions of His enemies occasion to His people!

Since Christ is set down on the right hand of the Majesty in heaven, with what awful reverence should we approach Him in the duties of His worship! Away with light and low thoughts of Christ! Away with formal, irreverent, and careless frames in praying, hearing, and speaking of Christ. Away with all deadness, and drowsiness in duties, for He is a *great King* with whom we have to do. A King to whom the kings of the earth are but as little bits of clay. Lo, the angels cover their faces in His presence. He is an adorable Majesty.

When John had a vision of this enthroned King, about sixty years after His ascension; such was the over-powering glory of Christ, *as the sun when it shineth in its strength*, that when he saw Him, he fell at His feet as dead, and he probably would have died if Christ had not laid His hand on him and said, "Fear not, I am the first and the last; I am he that liveth, and was dead, and behold I am alive for evermore" (Revelation 1:17–18). When He appeared to Saul on the way to Damascus, it was in glory above the glory of the sun, which overpowered him also, and laid him as one dead upon the ground.

Oh, that you did but know what a glorious Lord you worship and serve. Who makes the very place of His feet glorious, wherever He comes. Surely, He is greatly to be feared in the assembly of His saints, and to be held in reverence by all that are round about Him. There is indeed a boldness or free liberty of speech allowed to the saints, (see Ephesians 3:13). But no rudeness or irreverence is allowed. We may indeed come, as the children of a king come to their father who is both their awful sovereign and tender father. In this double relation there is no doubt a mixture of love and reverence in their hearts when they come into His presence. You may be *free*, but not *rude*, in His presence. Though He is your Father, Brother, and Friend; yet, the distance between you is infinite.

Since Christ is so gloriously advanced in the highest throne, then no one needs to reckon himself dishonored by suffering the vilest things for His sake. Someone has said, "It is no disgrace for us to suffer what Christ suffered, nor is it any glory for you to do what Judas did." The very chains and sufferings of Christ have glory in them. Hence Moses "esteemed the very reproaches of Christ greater riches than the treasures of Egypt" (Hebrews 11:26). He saw an excellency in the very worst things of Christ, in His reproaches and sufferings, that made him leap out of his honors and riches into them. He did not (as one says) only *endure the reproaches of Christ*, but counted them *treasures* to be reckoned among His honors and things of value. So Thuanus reports of Ludovicus Marsacus, a noble knight of France, when he was led with other martyrs, who were bound with cords, to execution. In his dignity he was not bound, for he cried, "give me my chain too, let me be a knight of the same order." Disgrace itself is honorable, when it is endured for the *Lord of Glory*. And surely there is a little paradise, a young heaven, in sufferings for Christ. If there were nothing else in it, but that they are endured on His account, it would richly reward all we can endure for Him. If we consider how exceedingly kind Christ is to those who count it their glory to be abased for Him, that though He is always kind to His people, He overcomes himself in kindness when they suffer for Him, it would make people love His reproaches.

Since Christ did not sit down to rest in heaven until He had finished His work on earth, then it is in vain for us to think of rest until we have finished our work as Christ also did His. How willing are we to find rest here! To dream of that, which Christ never found in this world, nor any ever found before us. Oh, think not of resting until you have finished working and sinning. Your life and your labors must end together. "Write [saith the Spirit] blessed are the dead that die in the Lord, for they rest from their labors" (Revelation 14:13). Here you must have the *sweat* and there the *sweet*. It is too much to have two heavens. Here you must be content to dwell in the *tents of Kedar*; hereafter you shall be *within the curtains of Solomon*. Heaven is the place of which it may be truly said that *there the weary be at rest*. Oh think not of sitting down on this side of heaven. There are four things that will keep the saints from sitting down on earth to rest: grace, corruption, devils, and wicked people.

1. Grace will not allow you to rest here. Its tendencies are beyond this world. It will be looking and longing for the blessed hope. A gracious person takes himself for a pilgrim seeking a better country, and is always suspicious of danger in every place and state. He is still beating up the sluggish heart with such language as "Arise, depart, this is not thy rest, for it is polluted" (Micah 2:10). Its further tendencies and continual jealousies will keep you from sitting long still in this world.

2. Your corruptions will keep you from rest here. They will continually test your spirit and keep you upon your watch. Saints have their hands filled with work by their own hearts everyday—sometimes to prevent sin and sometimes to lament it, but always to watch and fear, to mortify and kill sin. Sin will not long allow you to be quiet.

3. If a bad heart will not break your rest here, then a busy devil will do it. He will find you work enough with his temptations and suggestions, and unless you can sleep quietly in his arms as the wicked do, there is no rest to be expected. "Your adversary, the devil, goeth about as a roaring lion, seeking whom he may devour; whom resist" (1 Peter 5:8).

4. The devil's servants and instruments will not let you be quiet on this side of heaven. Their very name speaks their turbulent disposition. "My soul, [saith the holy man] is among lions, and I lie even among them that are set on fire, even the sons of men, whose teeth are spears and arrows" (Psalm 62:4). Well then, be content to enter into your rest, as Christ did into His. He sweat, then He sat, and so must you.

Christ Our Communion

This blessed table is "the Lord's Table." It is not the table of any particular church or congregation; it is the banquet which the Lord of glory provides for His subjects, which the Father of mercies spreads for His sons and daughters, to which the Redeemer bids His disciples, that their love may be rekindled, and their faith increased; and where the Holy Spirit reveals to the faithful the treasures which are hid in Emmanuel! In rightly partaking of this banquet we look back to the 'full, perfect, and sufficient sacrifice' made for sinners, when our Savior Jesus Christ cried on the cross: "It is finished." We look up, and by faith behold the living Redeemer, who sustains the life that He hath given; and we look onward to that glorious hour when the marriage of the Lamb shall be consummated, and His blood-bought bride shall sit down at the heavenly feast, amidst the anthems of unnumbered angels and in the radiance of her Father's presence. 'Blessed are they that are called to the marriage supper of the Lamb.' "

W. Pennefather

7
The Food of the Soul

*T*he cup of blessing, which we bless, is it not the communion of the blood of Christ? The bread which we break, is it not the communion of the body of Christ? For we, being many, are one bread and one body, for we are all partakers of that one bread" (1 Corinthians 10:16–17).

Life and food are dependent upon each other. The nature of the life decides the character of the food. The lion eats flesh, and the ox eats grass, each according to its nature. On the other hand, the character of the food will decide the growth, the strength, and the increase of the life. You know that in food there are very different elements of nourishment. A medical man will give to one what will strengthen the bones, if they be weak; he has another sort of food for the person who needs muscle. The food will decide the character and the strength of the life.

What is the food we need for our immortal spirits? We need the body and the blood of the Son of God. Oh, mystery of mysteries that Jesus says, "I came from heaven to give my flesh to be the life of the world!" Surely it is of consequence that we understand rightly what this means. I must not only look upon Christ as the bread of my life, but especially upon the broken body and the shed blood—upon the dying Christ. The death of Christ must be my chief nourishment.

The Chief Glory of Christ

Let us look at this. You know that the death of Christ is His chief characteristic. He came from heaven with a commandment from the Father that He should lay down His life. Christ lived His whole life in the spirit of preparation, offering himself for death as the consummation of His work. He died! Without His obedient sacrificial death, He never could have risen again, nor have ascended to the throne. In heaven, He still reminds us: "I am he that liveth and was dead, and I am alive for evermore." Through eternity, He is on the throne as the Lamb that was slain, and the saints never cease singing of the preciousness of His blood. "Thou hast purchased us unto God by thy blood!" Brother, the chief glory of Christ is His death.

If I am to feed upon Christ, I must especially feed upon His death. What does that mean? Look at it a moment. For instance, plants, trees, and flowers have a certain food prepared and put into the soil for them. Take something so simple as bone fertilizer—in the bone you have an external substance into which the plant inserts its rootlets, passing through all the little cells of the bone and taking out from it its very life-essence. It does not take up a single grain of the substance itself, but it takes the very essence of what is in the bone. This it works up into the sap; and then the spirit that is in the plant, received from the food in the soil, creates the leaves, the flowers, and the fruit in their beauty. In the same manner, our bodies take what the medical doctor prescribes to meet the weakness in our constitution—some preparation with different elements in it, but we take it all in one. There it is, but we take it and it disappears; it enters our blood; its life elements enter into and become one with our life and strengthen our frame.

How can I feed on the death of Christ? Feeding upon a thing means taking its inmost essence into your being. When I feed on meat, or on bread, or on anything else, I take its life-power into my constitution. And what does it now mean, feeding upon the body and blood of Jesus? Let me give you a few thoughts, very simple and short. I must find out what the death of Christ signifies and what its inmost spirit is. By faith, I must then accept it, and appropriate it, and look up to Jesus to work it within me in His divine power.

The Meaning of the Death of Christ

Now, what does the death of Christ mean? First, what does it mean in its *relation to sin*? It means that Christ counted sin an accursed thing; and He was willing to give His life to get our life out from under the curse of sin. When I feed upon the death of Christ, it means that I count sin an accursed thing. I acknowledge that sin has power over the whole of my natural life. I consent to say, "I want to die away from sin." There is no separation from sin but by death; and I want the power of Christ's death to work in me that I may be made free from sin. That is what the apostle teaches us in Romans six.

Have you ever noticed how both baptism and the Lord's Supper have to do with nothing but the death of Christ? Now, how can I live so that I do not continue in sin? Just know that you are baptized into the death of Christ, and then feed upon His death. That means that I accept the terrible curse of all sin. I accept the proof that all my life is under the power of sin, and that there is no way of getting rid of it but by the absolute death in Christ.

Next, what did Christ's death mean in *relation to the world*? It meant this: Christ and the world met each other; and in the temptation in the wilderness, the Prince of the world tried to effect a compromise, a reconciliation between Christ and the world. Christ was not, however, of the world, and He would not have a kingdom of this world. The controversy was settled on Calvary. There Christ allowed the world to crucify Him, to prove that it was in irreconcilable enmity to Him. Christ's death means this: The world hates me because I am not of it; I am crucified to the world and the world to me.

And now, if I feed upon the death of Jesus Christ—the broken body and the shed blood—this means that I want to take this element of the crucifixion up into my spiritual life. This element is separation from the world, antagonism to the world; it means to be crucified to the world and to have the world crucified to me. That made Paul glory in the Cross. It was not only atonement and it was not only pardon, glorious as these gifts are, but he gloried in the fellowship of the Cross.

Oh! dear friends, let us long for it. The world that we live in is the world that rejected Christ. The world will have nothing to do with the rule of Christ as King. Let us follow Christ and go out of the camp. And as we feed upon His body and blood, let this be our prayer, *"Oh, my Father, may the Spirit which was in Christ when He died on the Cross— separation from the world—may the spirit of Christ's death dwell with me."* As I said before, of that on which I feed I take out its life elements and absorb them into my constitution. That is what I do in my participation of the body and blood of Christ in its separation from the world. I want the death of Christ to be the ruling power of my whole being.

Look at the death of Christ again in its *relation to God.* He gave up His own will to the will of the Father forever.

116

Unparalleled humility made Him say, "I am nothing, and God is all." Humility made Him willing to die. In humility, He declared: "My will as compared with the will of God shall never be of any value. I give up my will, I give up myself to be nothing; God must be all." That was the spirit of Christ's death. And when I say, "Oh Jesus, feed me with Your broken body and with Your shed blood," it means nothing less than to say, "Let the dispositions, the inclinations, and the tempers which urged You on to Calvary dwell in me, my Lord. I want to feed upon Your death; let that become the nutriment and the characteristic of my life."

Beloved, are you perhaps struggling against the outbreaks of your own will and your pride? Are you still at times self-willed, battling with God? Are you seeking exaltation in any shape? I pray you today, come feed upon the broken body and the shed blood of the Lamb of God, who in meekness and lowliness of heart, humbled himself and became obedient unto death. Humility, obedience to God, surrender to God's will—this is the secret of Gethsemane and of Calvary.

"Oh Jesus, feed us today! Feed us with the heavenly bread, the body and the blood which are the proof and power of Your most blessed and complete surrender to the will of God, of Your divine and most perfect humility."

Once more, what is the death of Christ in its *relation to us*? He died for us. Yes, you cannot partake of the death of Christ without remembering His dying love to lost sinners. What moved Him to come to die? He did not need it for himself. He did not need to bear the curse, to be crucified to the world, and to give up His will to the Father. The inspiration of it all was love to us. And if I am going to feed upon a crucified Christ, I must be prepared, I must be hungry, I must have a heart that longs to have this element of the heavenly food enter my being.

I must be ready to give up myself, like Jesus, to live and die for my fellowmen. I am not come here to eat food for my mere enjoyment. Verily, no: food from heaven to strengthen me for heaven's work; food from Calvary to strengthen me for Calvary's work; the crucified Christ that I may be fitted to carry the crucified Christ in my life to my fellow men.

Brethren, you all know how Paul reminds us that we are "to show forth the Lord's death until he come." How am I to do that? By thinking of it, and speaking of it, and trusting in it, and eating and drinking in commemoration? Yes, but that is not all. I am to show the death of the Lord in my body, in my life. That is showing forth the death of the Lord. You know those words of Paul so well, "carrying about the dying of the Lord Jesus in the body, that the life of Jesus may be made manifest." How can you make manifest the life of Christ? By having the death of Christ working in you. You know that when Paul had been more than twenty years an apostle, as an aged man he still cried, "I count all things but loss, if I may know him . . . in the fellowship of his sufferings, being made conformable to his death."

In chapter three, we spoke about the new and living way. Is not that it? You long, like Jesus, to die for your fellow men. Come, eat this bread and drink this wine that the power of the death of Christ may get possession of you. And as often as you eat, as often as you drink, do this in remembrance of Him, of what He was and what He can make you to be. Show forth the Lord's death until He comes. God grant that each time you partake of the Lord's Supper, it may increasingly become the power of Christ's death in your spirit and life!

Trust in Jesus Christ

Just two words in conclusion. You may say, "Ought not the Communion to be a feast of joy and gladness?" It ought to be. But you think, "What you speak is dark and depressing." Ah no, brother, it is not. My message is one of resurrection joy. Where is resurrection joy to be had but at the grave of Jesus? Sink into the death of Jesus. Carry about His dying in your inmost heart. Strike the roots of your being deep into the grave of Jesus and become nothing, so the joy of God and the resurrection of life shall dwell in you. It is not depressing to hear of death with Jesus; it is our joy and gladness that there is a way open for us out of self and its power into the life of Jesus himself.

And then the other thought I want to give you is this: Oh, be not anxious about how you will be able to realize all these elements of the death of Christ in your life! When your body is in a healthy state, you spend your half-hour in taking breakfast or lunch, and then your part of the job is done. God has ordered everything so that the assimilation of nutriment goes on quietly without any effort on your part and without your noticing it. You rise from the table and go to your work; you spend hours in business and never think again about what is going on in your blood to strengthen your bones and muscles. The assimilation of the food is a work of infinite importance, but it goes on quietly, surely, without thought or effort. Even so, when you come to feed upon the broken body and shed blood, quietly and restfully trust Jesus, by His Holy Spirit, to make it real in you. The eating is your work; the inward assimilation is God's work. Just open up your whole being and say, "Lord, one favor above all others—the chief of Your blessings! Oh, for the power of Your death in my life!"

I know there are Christians who fear that in our days (there is indeed too much reason for such fear) the Church of Christ knows too little of His crucifixion, the fellowship of His suffering—rejection and separation from everything that is of the world and the natural life. Oh, believer, trust

Christ to teach you; yield yourself to Him. Feed much upon His death. He will give you life out of death. He will, in divine power, be your life. And then, as each one seeks fellowship with the crucified Christ, we shall all have fellowship one with another. Praise God! We shall all have fellowship in one bread and prove that we are one body. Nearness to Christ will draw us nearer to each other.

We said in the beginning that the food was the life. Let it be so now. We have been fed with heavenly bread; let our lives be very heavenly. God help us, brothers and sisters! Let us lead heavenly lives; let us, in the death of Jesus, die to the spirit of the world and live the heavenly life. He will do it for us. We have not eaten of this bread alone, but all together—one bread. Let all hearts overflow in love to each other. Let us pray today, and unceasingly, the prayer that God would bind all His children throughout the world in the bond of the love of Christ and of His Holy Spirit. Let us so pass through this world, showing forth the death of the Lord "until he come." He is coming in His glory. But until He come, let us show forth His first coming—His death for the world and victory over sin. God help us! Amen.

"The Table of the Lord is a golden link, uniting the two great facts of the Bible—that fact of history, the first advent of Jesus Christ, and that fact of prophecy, His second coming again. The Table of the Lord is retrospective: it takes our minds back to the Cross—we are to 'show forth his death.' And it is prospective: 'till He come.' Thus, the two ends of our own salvation are united together by this Table of Memorial. We have the first end of salvation now; we are waiting for its final end—the glorious consummation. Like the stars in the heavens, which speak and yet there is no audible voice, the dumb elements of bread and wine speak to our hearts today. And our souls are kept in equipoise by the exercise of memory and hope."—*Rev. George C. Needham*

"Wherefore, holy brethren, partakers of the heavenly calling, consider the Apostle and High Priest of our profession, Christ Jesus" (Hebrews 3:1).